A Book of Insight

Wisdom From the Other Side

A Book of
Insight

Wisdom From the Other Side

Tilde Cameron & Tina Fiorda

Stone Circle Publishing

www.abookofinsight.com

Library and Archives Canada Cataloguing in Publication

Cameron, Tilde, 1963-
    A book of insight : wisdom from the other side / Tilde Cameron & Tina Fiorda.

ISBN 978-0-9813145-0-1

    1. Spiritualism. 2. Guides (Spiritualism). 3. Reality. I. Fiorda, Tina, 1955-
II. Title.

BF1272.C34 2009   133.9'1   C2009-904630-X

Cover design by Nathaniel McAnally

Stone Circle Publishing
British Columbia,
Canada

www.stonecirclepublishing.com

Ouija is a registered trademark owned by Hasbro, Inc.

Acknowledgements

Tina & Tilde would like to thank the following people:

Linda Fiorda. Mom, thank you for your unwavering love and support.

Ian Cameron, for your love, patience, and continued support.

Paul Gruenwald, for your timely introductions and assistance.

John M. Gray and Ian Ferguson, for your advice and words of wisdom.

Karen Delaney-Wolverton, for your continued friendship and generosity.

Valerie Fawkes-Kim, for your feedback and support.

Anna Skokan and Annette Ducharme, for your friendship, fun, and laughter.

And finally, we'd like to thank Melanie, Em, and Demna for imparting their words of wisdom.

Dedication

This book is lovingly dedicated to our father, Giuseppe Fiorda. You are forever alive within our hearts.

The following pages contain the question and answer dialogue that took place between the authors and their spirit guides; Melanie, Em, and Demna.

Contents

Authors' Introductions

Tina Fiorda

My experiences began a long time ago, and I trust that they will continue. My earliest memories date back to the first few years of my life. As a baby, I remember the deep blue walls of my family's kitchen. At the age of two, I can remember lying in my crib, peering through the bars at my sleeping parents.

But I have other memories also, of laying in bed at night and mentally asking my friends to step out from the darkness of the walls to entertain me until I fell asleep. And they would. I have memories of floating down the stairs at night while the house slept. Or were they dreams?

I have always been a dreamer. I believe that dreams are the spring board to reality; a reality that is rich, and full, and mystical. Because of my experiences, I have developed a curiosity towards things I cannot see and a thirst to discover what else lies out there. What is reality all about? How does it operate? And what lies beyond the reality that we know?

My family moved from Toronto to Vancouver when I was thirteen years old, settling with my maternal grandparents, along with my mother's brother and sister for the first two years. That is when I saw a Ouija board for the first time. It may have belonged to my aunt or uncle. At that time it was regarded as a parlor game, and it aroused my curiosity.

It is not a parlor game. It is real, and it should be respected; to be used only in a positive and loving way. My sister and I surround ourselves with white light whenever we use the Ouija board; repeating a prayer of protection to God, our guides, and our angels. The book you are about to read was channeled entirely through the Ouija board.

I began playing around with the Ouija board over twenty years ago, and my sister joined in when she was old enough to participate. At first it was for sheer fun and curiosity. We knew nothing of protection prayers and engaged in silly games with it, trying to see if we could contact people like Janis Joplin or Marilyn Monroe. We soon realized that the Ouija board was an instrument to be respected. Over the years my sister and I have developed a relationship with our guides, Melanie, Em, and Demna, through it.

We began searching for answers about life and the dilemmas in our lives. Tilde and I discussed how cool it would be to use the Ouija board to attempt to channel material that would be relevant to a wider audience. Then one day in 2004, it happened. We were using the board, and the planchette took over and began spewing out material that we had not requested. When it was finished, we had a page on meditation. We were impressed, but for some reason we put it aside until the summer of 2007. At that time we began to think about the page on meditation and felt the need to continue from where we had left off. In July of that year, Tilde and I began to work with the Ouija board again, and the result is a book of insight that amazes us beyond belief. We are truly blessed to be able to share this book with you and hope that it will ignite a spark deep within your soul.

A Book of Insight opens our minds to the possibility that there is a deeper sense and purpose for us as a loving, unified whole. It shows us how we are all interconnected and introduces us to the possibilities of alternate realities. It offers insights to our emotions, existence, and to our probable future.

We hope that you will enjoy your journey through this book regardless of how you view its content and delivery. Our hope is that the message resonates within your soul.

Tilde Cameron

When my sister and I first started playing with a Ouija board, I never in my wildest dreams could have imagined that it would one day be delivering material to us that would eventually become a book. I am still amazed by this.

I must have been about sixteen years old the first time we started playing with a Ouija board. Nothing would ever really happen, but every now and then we would pull out the board and try again. It wasn't until around three years after my initial encounters with the Ouija board that it actually started "speaking" to us. It would usually take a few minutes for our spirit friends to arrive, and the messages would come through very slowly. I can't remember what the messages were, but they would have been centered around questions about boyfriends, social events, and what they could predict in our futures. We didn't take any of this very seriously at the time, but we certainly found it entertaining.

It wasn't long after this that we would meet our spirit guides for the first time. Melanie introduced herself to me as my spirit guide. From what she has told me, she and I have guided each other through various lifetimes. We all have spirit guides; some of us have many at one time. I find it comforting to know that we are being looked after and guided throughout our various lifetimes.

After our initial introduction to our guides, we noticed that the messages started becoming more interesting and of a spiritual nature. I have always been fascinated by the "other side" and all things unseen, even though I still found them to be somewhat frightening. As a child, I had a few unexplainable experiences and visions, even waking up one night to find a female apparition sitting in a chair beside my bed, looking down at me. Needless to say, that experience startled me enough that I threw the covers over my head and didn't emerge again until the next morning. Thankfully, she was gone when I awakened, but did come back to visit one more time after that. Although I have never understood this experience and the others I have had, I was still fascinated by them and wanted to explore them further.

I have always been an avid reader, and the majority of books I've read have been focused on spiritual and metaphysical subjects. Who are we, where did we come from, and what is our purpose here? These are just a few of the questions that I've sought answers to, and I know that I am not alone in my search. Much of humanity has asked these same questions and wondered if there is more meaning behind our lives and our day to day experiences than we are aware of.

Although I do not consider myself to be psychic, I think that these experiences, and many more that I have had, make me a little more "sensitive" than some people, and perhaps this is why I am able to channel my spirit friends. You and I all have this "sensitivity" or sixth sense, as it is often referred to, but it is more developed in some people than in others. Having said that, all of us can further develop this sensitivity if we are so inclined. Like anything else, it just takes focus and practice.

As we continued with our Ouija sessions, we would find ourselves being visited by relatives or friends who had crossed over to the other side. At this point, we still weren't fully trusting of the entities that were coming through or the messages we were receiving. It's not that the messages were of a negative nature. Quite contrary to that, the messages were usually very positive and uplifting. The problem was that we were still dealing with the unknown, and this made us somewhat nervous at times. And then there was the constant questioning between Tina and me; "Are you moving it? No, I'm just following it. Are you moving it? No, I'm not moving it. Are you sure you're not moving it?"

As a disclaimer, I feel it is important to mention that Tina and I always say a prayer of protection before we begin a session. We truly are dealing with many things unknown, and just as there is both positive and negative in the three dimensional world we live in, there is also both positive and negative on the other side. We have absolutely no interest in encountering any of the negative and are, therefore, always very careful. I strongly caution anyone considering using a Ouija board to say prayers of protection and to surround themselves in white light before going ahead. It is important to have only positive intentions if using a Ouija board.

Now, fast forward to September of 2004. Tina and I sat down for one of our sessions, and our guides began dictating a couple of paragraphs worth of material on meditation. They then proceeded to tell us that they had started dictation on our book. This was quite a surprise to both of us, but we were intrigued at the thought of our guides channeling a book through us.

Now, fast forward again to summer of 2007. Tina and I were having a conversation about "that book our guides started writing," and how maybe we should have another session to see if they wanted to continue with it. For some reason we hadn't continued with it at the time, and as time went on, had almost forgotten about it entirely. So, we sat down for a session, and just as if no time had passed, our guides continued on with the material on meditation. It was incredible! Almost three full years had passed, and they just picked up right where they had left off. It was seamless.

We were amazed by the material they were dictating to us. We had no idea what the book would be about. They had given us a book title and the title of the first chapter. Other than that, and being told that the book would contain sixteen chapters, we didn't know what the other chapters would be titled or what the subject matter would be. It wasn't until they completed dictation of the chapter we were working on, that they would give us the title of the next chapter. Letter by letter and word for word, it would come through. Because of the "choppy" way it was being delivered to us, we would only have a sense of what they were writing about. It wasn't until we would play the recording back (we speak the words they spell out, into a digital recorder), type it all out, and then read it back, that we really knew what they had delivered. Each time we read the material, we were blown away by the information. It wasn't until we were half way through the book that we finally started trusting that our guides were really delivering this material, and that it wasn't one of us cheating and moving the pointer. We always joke that neither one of us is creative enough to come up with this stuff.

At times, the information we received was so "out there," that we questioned whether or not we should include it in the book. What would our readers think? Would it be too esoteric or sound too bizarre to digest? In the end, we decided to leave everything in, and let you, the reader, decide for yourself.

And here we are now, with our first book in hand. I still find it hard to believe at times, but here it is. I hope that you will read it with an open mind and enjoy it as much as we enjoyed this peculiar process of writing it.

I wish you all love and enlightenment.

Introduction

We are not of the physical world, but we know your physical world better than you do, for our vantage point is one that spans the physical and spiritual. We are what you refer to as guides, and we are Tina and Tilde's guides. We are Demna, Em, and Melanie, but we also encompass other guides who would speak through us to you.

We have been with the writers since their births, but we have known each other for an eternity. As guides, we have guided, protected, and watched over Tina and Tilde throughout their current lifetime. We are of the unseen and spiritual realm and have a vested interest in the future of mankind.

As children, the writers have had many experiences of the other realm that have confused them at times, but sparked their interest in the spiritual realm. We have been here throughout to guide their spiritual growth and provide answers through coincidence and synchronicity.

When the writers first began their practice with the Ouija board, it was more for fun and curiosity than it was for true communication with us. As time progressed and they became more seriously immersed in their spiritual quests, the tone of their interactions with Ouija became more serious and spiritually inquisitive. When we felt that they were ready, we began the first transmission of this book. It was in 2004.

Meditation is the most spiritual connection and form of communication with the Source, so we began with meditation as the first chapter. We urge all of mankind to meditate on a daily basis. It is the one most important thing you can do for your spiritual awakening, hence the first page we channeled was on meditation.

After three years of hiatus, the writers began to continue work on this book. It is an important book of insight for the human race, and we have kept its format and delivery simple and concise as to be understood by all readers. We felt that Tina and Tilde were ready for the roles they assumed before they birthed onto this planet and into this reality. Their lifetime quest has been in pursuit of spiritual knowledge, and this has been a part of their continuing journey into the realm of what you would deem the spiritual unknown.

We have chosen to come forth at this time because mankind has reached a crossroads at this time in his development, and he must choose the path that will affect the balance of his evolution. Mankind has the ability and power to destroy himself, along with the planet that sustains him, and this is the most important crossroad of his development.

We have chosen these writers because it was determined before their births into this realm, and the time is upon us now. We have a loving vested interest in you, and thus, we have chosen to deliver the message unto you. Your Earth is in peril of becoming a wasteland, and you must activate yourselves in the loving spirit of whence you came.

Many messengers have been among you to deliver knowledge and many more are emerging today. From the early days of Nostradamus and before, there have been sages and prophets among you. At this time, the quantity is expanding, and there are more messengers coming to Earth to awaken mankind.

We love you; for we are all one, of and within the Source, and our hope is that you will read this book along with the many others that would impart spiritual awakening. Our intent is to save mankind from a fate that is not meant for his spiritual connection. We would wish you light and love and would make your journey through this book enlightening.

In light and in love, we wish you a joyous awakening.

Chapter One:

Meditation

Melanie: Meditation has been used for over thousands of your Earth years as a tool of spiritual focus and mental detachment from the physical world that you dwell in. It is your spiritual connection to your Source and inner self. Many sages, prophets, medicine men, and shamans have utilized this tool over the ages to connect themselves with the world of the unseen spiritual realm. It is the quintessential tool that you can utilize for connecting to your inner self and listening inward to the guidance of your inner soul and Divine Source from whence you came.

Your sages and priests of ancient times understood the spiritual connection that meditation provided, and they utilized this tool to connect them with their spiritual guides and Source for the purpose of attaining information and valuable guidance. Liken it to a teacher that awaits upon the student to request guidance and knowledge. These ancient shamans and such, understood that the process of meditation allowed them to commune with ancient masters and guides. They utilized this meditation time to acquire the knowledge that they sought through a connective merging with the

Source energy. On this plane, they could receive direct information and knowledge that they could then utilize for the greater good of their people and patients.

This knowledge is available to all that seek it and will take the time and dedication to follow its path. This knowledge is understood on the soul level. It is on a level that we would term as the inner knowing. It has no words attached, for words are utilized by mankind to operate within his three dimensional world. Spirit has no need of words, for knowledge is understood on the level of the soul.

Your sages and medicine men, as well as spiritual advisors of your past, utilized meditation as a tool to anchor themselves in the spiritual realm prior to healing and religious ceremonies. In those ancient times, religious ceremonies had more to do with nature and spirit than the religious ceremonies of today, which are basically just practiced rituals. Your ancestors understood that there was an unseen world, and that meditation was one of the methods of connecting with this world.

Em: Your divinity is directly connected to your God Source through meditation. It is the portal that mankind has to his divine self. Think of this portal as a direct line of connection and communication. You are wired to receive and transmit conscious thought through this connection. It is the manner in which you can receive and commune with your God Source, and it truly is such a simple concept.

It is through the oneness with the Source that this occurs. There is no separation between mankind and his Source other than the separation he perceives in his mind chatter. When you are in a meditative state, this mind chatter eventually subsides, and you will begin to perceive a manner of tranquility and union with this energy. We call this the mankind/Source connection.

Through meditation, you can maintain a centeredness in your life that can help you to guide your course and steer your ship as you journey through your lifetime on this planet that you call home.

Meditation is the most powerful tool that you have at your disposal for connections of many kinds; and by this, we mean connections to your God Source as well as with other minds on your planet and beyond, into other realms that you are only beginning to discover. By this, we are referring to the psychic connection with other minds and with the spiritual realm.

It is through meditation that you can begin to develop your psychic communication abilities. There are many examples of this, and mankind has only to open his awareness and he will begin to notice a world of possibilities. There are many gifted people on your planet who utilize these abilities for many beneficial outcomes. They are able to communicate with the spiritual realm on behalf of grieving people, thus helping them to understand that their loved ones have not died, but have passed on to another level of reality. You, yourselves, use this ability many times without being aware of it. Remember the times when you have thought of someone only to have the phone ring and discover that this person is calling. If mankind would meditate on a daily basis, these lines of communication would become more developed.

Meditation is key to attracting many beneficial situations into your life. When you understand how reality operates, then you will begin to understand how to manipulate it. Many people feel that they are victims of a life that they have no control over, but in reality (pun intended), they are actually a victim of themselves and the reality that *they* have created.

Many people live their lives without understanding how their thoughts and feelings mold their day to day reality. They go through the process of living without thought as to how they actually create the reality they operate within. Many live their lives in an existence that they feel has been thrust upon them without realizing that they, themselves, are responsible for everything that is experienced in their existence. People are simply existing in a prison with invisible bars.

If you stop and take an inventory of your lives, you will begin to see that much that occurs to you is a result of the thoughts and beliefs that you hold about the reality of your existence. Your thoughts and beliefs can confine your life within a narrow framework that it then operates within. Meditation will help to expand your mind, thus allowing you to view the bigger picture of awareness.

There was a time in your history when mankind thought the world was flat. This confined him to his area of the world, for he thought that if he ventured too far he would fall off the planet. In this manner, you too are confined by beliefs that you believe to be absolute. If you would venture beyond your current beliefs, you will discover a world that you have been blind to. It is a freeing experience, and we urge you to open your minds.

Make a list of all the things you are unhappy with, and if you examine your beliefs, you will find that they confine you within a framework of beliefs that victimize you. All you need to do is change the way you perceive reality, and it will change almost without much effort.

Beliefs that are binding have a hold on you that you do not realize. Such beliefs can be classified as ideas about reality that are rigid in nature, and compounded upon each other, they become the prisons that contain you and prevent your progress in life. These beliefs range from an idea that may be a simple innocuous truth, to one such as the belief that your gender prevents you from progressing and attaining that which you desire. This is what we would term as a belief that binds you and prevents you from becoming all that you can be.

Make a list of beliefs that bind you and that you would like to change, and focus on a new set of beliefs that would replace these, and within a few weeks, you will notice changes that will affect you in a very positive way.

Always remember that meditation is the important key that will unlock and expose the new beliefs into your every day reality. Be conscious of your thoughts, for they have a reality of their own and will affect the outcome. If your thoughts are constantly negative, your day to day experiences will also be negative. When negative thoughts come into your mind, be aware of them consciously and immediately replace them with positive ones. Meditate every day on the new beliefs that you want to replace the old ones with, and then focus on making them a daily part of your life.

Through meditation, you will be able to relax your conscious mind, thus silencing the chatter of your ever present ego. This ego is what prevents many of you from going forth confidently in life to achieve the dreams that you would set for yourselves. Your ego is that part of your duality that ensures the survival of the individual and the survival of the species. It is reflected as the left brain chatter that continues daily within your mind.

The purpose of the ego is to reason and calculate within the dimension that you occupy. It is the part of each person that exists as the individual I. It is the unique personality that each person holds within himself. It is the individual I that separates each individual from the other within your dimension. If we eliminated the left brained ego, then mankind would simply perceive his oneness with the Source and merged identity. It is the ego that allows you to function and think logically within your world. It is the ego who is responsible for the instinctual conscious survival of each individual.

Through fear based thoughts, you are hindered by your ego at times, for it fears the consequences of the unknown factor in any given situation. This is a result of its need for survival. Fear of the unknown is a survival mechanism of the ego. Once your ego is still, your spiritual side can begin to acquire a sense of itself, and this part of you is connected to the divinity that birthed, powers, and guides your life through your intuitive nature. This is the part of you that knows its divine nature and fears not, the path it must choose. This is the part of you that will help to alter your beliefs in order to lead a more purposeful life.

A meditation period of as little as fifteen minutes a day will bring significant change into your life. The process of meditation is quite simple, and the preparation is just as simple. It is important to find a quiet, comfortable place where you can find peace and relaxation. A good way to do this is in a quiet, secluded, and safe spot where you can feel a better sense of being alone with yourself.

Wake up in the morning, and make it the first thing you do before you get out of bed. Set your alarm earlier than you would normally be up, and take this time to meditate. In the morning you are fresh from sleep and are more open to the new suggestions that you are planting in your mind. Meditate in a place where you feel safe and comfortable. It will make the process a better one. Make sure you do not lie down, for you will fall asleep which is not the plan.

The methods of meditation depend on which ever works best for you. Some people prefer to sit cross legged, while others prefer to sit with both feet planted firmly on the floor. Some people prefer to meditate with their eyes closed, while others prefer to focus on the flame of a candle in a dimly lit room. Discover the method that works best for you, as meditation has no stringent rules.

Make the room a comfortable setting by dimming it and lighting a candle. Sit in a comfortable place and position that will be conducive to a smoother flow. As you sit there, allow the thoughts to enter, and make sure that these thoughts flow without impediment. Be patient in the beginning, for many thoughts will occupy your mind. Be aware of these thoughts, and let them flow through your consciousness. Do not entertain them, but let them flow. Make sure that you do not dwell on them. Your mind is merely relieving itself of clutter, and in time they will dissipate. Once they dissipate, allow your mind to focus on the here and now. A stillness will descend upon you, and an awareness of the here and now will permeate your soul. It is within this powerful stillness that you can begin to influence powerful changes within your life. This is the moment when you can begin to adopt your new set of beliefs. Focus on that which you would like to attract, and visualize it as having a reality of its own. In this stillness you can make changes in your life and start affecting your future. As time goes on, and you become more proficient in the process, the experience will flow more smoothly.

Are you saying that just by visualizing that which we would like to attract, it will become manifested?

No. Visualization is but a step to reality. It is from dreams that reality springs forth. By dreams, we mean your intense desire. Visualization is a tool that is utilized for creating reality. One must integrate this with intense desire, visualization, and beliefs. These go hand in hand. If you have the visualization, but not the belief that you can acquire that which you desire, then you are merely engaging in wishful thinking. Visualize that which you desire, and put yourself in the scene; experience the emotions, the smells, the touch associated with the scene. Have the belief that this is your future desire being fulfilled, but most of all, have the belief in yourself. Believe that you are capable of manifesting it. Believe that you deserve it. Visualization is a component of the materialization of your desire. We can be there to guide you through the process. We are your unseen hands.

Who, or what, is it that we are connecting with in meditation, and what happens when we connect?

When you are in this still moment of now, you will become aware of a presence. This is the Source. This is your Source. It is the Universal Source that you and we are all connected to. At this time the stillness is so powerful as to be felt. It is a God Source. There are many names for God. You are connecting with your Source of Godness. Many would call it your Higher Self, All That Is, The Source, God, and many more. Many religions have different names than you for God, but it is all the same.

When you connect with the Source, you are opening a direct energy and spiritual line of communication and communion. It is this connection that helps guide your life and provides many answers to your questions. When you are connected to the Source, your line of communication is direct. It is not necessarily a verbal connection, but a connection on your deepest soul level. At this time your creative visualization can commence.

Make sure that your thoughts are pure. Make sure that your thoughts center around the positive changes that you want to make in your life. Do not use meditation to bring ill will upon others, for this illness will manifest itself upon you. At no time should meditation be used for this purpose.

When you are visualizing your changes, be sure to place yourself within this scene, and visualize yourself as you would want to become. This is the new version of your reality. Be sure to visualize the feelings attached to this new reality, and the people and places as well.

We will be there with you as your unseen facilitators. We are your guides and angels, and we love you. God loves you and wants you to be well and happy in his love.

Meditation, over time, will allow you to handle life situations and challenges more confidently. You will have an awareness that may have previously eluded you and a confidence that will surprise you.

This formula for meditation is a simple one, for truly there is no secret to it. Meditation is the ability to quiet your soul and gain entry to it. Make sure to take the time and do it every day. Fifteen minutes a day is as little as you need, and an hour a day is as much as you need.

There is no need to devote a major chapter to such a simple process.

Chapter Two:

Belief Systems

Melanie: Many belief systems occupy our minds about any given topic or situation in our lives. Beliefs can bind us or free us. We can be prisoners of these belief systems or we can be freed by them. In this chapter we will look at belief systems, and study how we can utilize them for our better good and personal growth.

Many times have we had desires in our lives, only to see them thwarted and dissipate. This is not because these desires are not attainable, but because the beliefs we hold around the manifestation of these desires thwarts or destroys their manifestation. Many of you are beholden to beliefs that are so engrained that you believe them to be facts of life. Many times have we experienced *success* because our beliefs have strong attachments to successful outcomes.

Em: From the time of our birth, we are beginning to view the world from our very unique perspective. The people who care for us begin to contribute to our perspectives through their own belief patterns and experiences. Then, as we develop and experience the world around us, we add to these observations which begin to mold our beliefs. By the time we are a year old, our minds begin to develop towards a fixed perception of truth. These truths are accepted as fact, and at no time do we question these perceived facts. Many facts, per se, accumulate throughout our lifetime and compound one upon the other. You are so attached to these beliefs that you do not know that there is another method of perception. Remember that beliefs are tied to perception and that perception affects the beliefs we hold, and we hold them dearly as if to lose them is to lose ourselves.

Can you elaborate a little more on how beliefs and perceptions are tied to one another? How do perceptions mold our beliefs?

Melanie: Perceptions are based on how we perceive something. That is, when we perceive or scrutinize something, how does it appear to us? Perception can be linked to the word "appearance" in this example. Based on the appearance of a thing or event, we tend to formulate thoughts or beliefs based on that which we perceive. We might perceive a storm to be calm; therefore, we create the thought or belief that the storm we are perceiving is rather calm and benign. In fact, we may be standing in the eye of a hurricane, and our perception is rather limited from our view point. The hurricane comes, and we realize that our perception was limited, and therefore, our belief surrounding the perception was limited to only a fragment of the entire reality of the hurricane.

In this way, our thoughts are limited because what we perceive on a day to day basis is only a part of the reality we are experiencing; therefore, it is important to understand that perception and thoughts are transitory at best because of the limitations we are dealing with in our reality. Our reality is limited to what we perceive of it; therefore, our thoughts are limited based on these perceptions. That is why meditation is so important. It opens our minds to the greater reality that we dwell in; therefore, expanding our perceptions, and therefore, expanding the possibilities of thoughts and beliefs.

So two people could be experiencing the same event, but based on how they are perceiving that event, they could be creating and experiencing two different realities.

Yes. If you think about it, that is entirely true. Our perceptions are filtered through our individual minds that have been individually molded based on our experiences and upbringing in our lives. Two people can see the same thing and perceive it differently thereby, creating different and individual beliefs about the same event.

If two different people are perceiving the same event differently, is one of them perceiving it correctly and the other incorrectly? Are they both right, or both wrong, or is it irrelevant?

No, they are not necessarily wrong. They just see different aspects of the same event. The person who sees the eye of the hurricane and perceives a mild storm is not wrong, for at that moment the storm is indeed calm. Another person would experience that same calmness and deduce that he is experiencing but a calm moment of a very savage storm. He perceives the storm as savage, not calm, but neither person is wrong in his perception. They simply translate the information differently based on their unique filters.

If our beliefs play a large role in creating our realties, and our perceptions help formulate our beliefs, should we change our perceptions in order to formulate the beliefs that would be most conducive to creating the reality we desire?

Yes, it would help because to hold on to a limited perception, while trying to change a belief about it, is sending out mixed signals. By altering your perception, or rather, by admitting that the perception you hold is not necessarily the only way to look at something, sets the stage for you to begin changing your belief about the perception.

Make sure to read this chapter with an open mind, and know that we are about to change your life.

Many of you are so attached to your beliefs that you have not the slightest conception that your entire life is the result of their existence in your mind and soul. No one is exempt. Your beliefs, at times, are so deeply rooted that you do not realize that you even have them. Beliefs can become so deeply rooted that they become invisible to you. It is when these beliefs become invisible that they become limiting in your lives because it is hard to change an aspect of your life when you are unaware of the beliefs you hold that are causing this limitation.

We would like you to examine all the beliefs you hold; even the ones you take for granted as absolute truths. Once you can identify all of your beliefs, you can begin to look at your lives and see how they have been affected by these beliefs.

You have spent a lifetime accumulating beliefs about everything that exists. Everything from ideas about people, things, nature. You are so entrenched that you don't know where to start to peel these layers away. We will show you the way.

Demna: You are guided by these beliefs that you hold. Many of your decisions are based on them. An example of this may be a simple decision to not apply for a job because you believe you are not qualified, but in reality the qualifications you have may be substantial to your prospective employer because he is governed by his own unique set of beliefs; so you see, it is all a matter of perception.

Beliefs, as you see, guide your decisions, and your decisions affect your reality which in turn has a direct impact on your life. By making an adjustment in your belief system, you can change the course of your life; and this adjustment can change many aspects, not only of *your* life, but the lives of those who are within your sphere due to our interconnectedness. You see, because we are all connected to each other through the Universal Source, our decisions, which are based on our beliefs, have a domino effect that ripples out throughout the world. How can my beliefs affect the world, you may ask? Simply take a look at the world events, and they speak for themselves. Do you think that these events are all random occurrences? They are not. So in order to affect not only your life, but a planetary change, it is important to change your beliefs and perceptions about reality.

Your beliefs about any given event or situation, lead to making decisions about how to react to them because your beliefs lead to conclusions which cause you to act upon these conclusions. Many of the events occurring in your world are the result of your active response. Your wars occur as a response to situations that instigate these events. Let meditation guide you in your day to day decisions, and you may in turn build a better world. Make your beliefs guide your heart to better results.

Many times have we altered our course in life by changing our beliefs and seen the difference in our lives and the lives of those around us. Many times have we been cured of a disease because of our internal shift. Maybe in some cases it has taken a life altering experience to shift someone's awareness. We will attempt to make that shift within you by avoiding the life altering experience to make it so. You can change your life practically over night, and that is what we will attempt to do.

Melanie: Many of you have a lot of questions at this point. We will attempt to clarify perceptions and beliefs as to how they relate to our interconnectedness.

Imagine a grid, if you will, and imagine this grid consisting of lines that intersect and connect to each other. Then imagine that we are this grid, and the points of intersection are the points where we are connected. If a connection point should be warped or broken, it will affect the points that it is connected to. If the lines of connection begin to warp or bend, it also affects the other lines of connection. In this manner, we too are connected, and our beliefs have a ripple effect to our connections. In this manner the entire planet is connected; not only humans, but all of the planet in its entirety. Left to our own unchecked random impulses, this planet could easily fall into disrepair.

You can, literally, not only change your beliefs and perceptions in a manner that would affect your life, but the life of the planet itself. Maybe, if you took a look around you at the world events, you could begin to see how the mass beliefs we share have brought about the world events that are causing so much grief and sadness. You can affect a change, but first it is important to see how we have cooperated in the state of our world.

You have created the world through cooperative mass beliefs. An example of this could be presented very simply. Let's take a local event such as an election. Your elected candidate had beliefs of his own that constituted the platform he ran on. He convinced the voters of his beliefs and convinced enough of them to get elected. The mass shared beliefs allowed a change to occur, and therefore, he was elected. Once elected, he put his beliefs into action which affected the events in his constituency which in turn affected the people he represented. If you can expand on this theory into the greater realm of the world we inhabit, you can see how this happens on a world level. Many scenarios are taking place at once and affecting changes and situations world wide.

We can alter our beliefs at any time to affect change in our lives. We can do this almost over night. Make a list of your beliefs. It can be a list of any beliefs you hold. Examine these beliefs. Are they holding you back or are they moving you forward? Are they making you happy or are they making you sad? Do you want to change them? Do you want to retain them?

Em: Have faith in this process, for we would like to bring positive changes to your life. We have a clarity that we would like to share with you.

Your beliefs can range from something as simple as a belief that you are tall or a belief that you are a failure. A

14

belief about being tall is not too terribly limiting, but a belief that you are a failure can be devastating.

Make a list of your beliefs, and make it as long as you want. You will begin to notice how these beliefs have affected your life. Have these beliefs harmed you? Have these beliefs aided you? Are these beliefs responsible for your current level of income? Are they responsible for your current position in life? Do you want to hold onto them? Do you want to replace them? Do you want to change your life? We believe that you do or you would not be reading this, and you would not have been asking yourself these very questions.

Think about the changes you want to make in your life, and think about how your beliefs have landed you where you are now.

We are going to do a belief altering exercise. Make a list of the beliefs you hold that you would like to shift. We spoke about this in the first chapter on meditation. List every belief that has binded you and held you back from your course in life. Dwell on these beliefs, and think back on how they have gotten you to this point. Have you held on to them too tightly? Would you like to replace them and affect a positive change in your life? We think so.

On a separate sheet of paper, write the set of beliefs you would like to adopt. If you would like to sell houses, but believe that you are not a good sales person, then your new belief would be, "I am a great sales person;" "I am a great real estate agent." Do this, and list all the beliefs you would like to adopt. Once your list is complete, read it out loud to yourself. Make it a habit to read them before you go to sleep at night, and make it the first thing you meditate on in the morning. Do this consistently every day for at least twenty one days, and no less. You will begin to notice a change in your reality and in your attitude, but most importantly, you will realize that you will begin to adopt these new beliefs as your new set of truths. You are now well on your way to changing your life.

Melanie: In time you will notice an internal change, and your beliefs will change also. The beliefs you are meditating on will become your truths, and your previous beliefs will seem foreign to you. This is only the beginning of your journey.

Em: Have faith in this journey, for there will be many good changes through practice and application. Be prepared to do the work, but most of all, be prepared and open to adopting your new set of beliefs and making them a part of your new reality. Not one thought should be entertained that will hold you back, for thoughts are real and will propel themselves towards manifestation.

How can thoughts be so powerful, and how do they propel themselves towards manifestation?

Melanie: Thoughts are especially powerful when the emotions that propel them are powerful. If you think about something with deep conviction, take a look inside yourself at the emotions that are attached. Do you ever find yourself daydreaming or thinking about something, and begin to have emotions attached as if the dream were a real event? That is the power of your emotion coupled with the thought that gives it energy that can propel it forward. If you ever, at one time, dreamt of becoming something and attached intense emotions of desire to it, you may have discovered at some future point, that your desire became manifested. This is the power of thought and emotion because both have energy attached, and energy propels itself towards manifestation. When manifestation does not occur, you need to examine your thoughts and fears surrounding your desires and dreams.

It sounds to me like it's really important to be aware of your emotions because they can either help you or hinder you.

Yes, they can. The emotion of fear surrounding a desired event, can hinder that event from manifesting. An emotion of excitement, and expectation, and great joy surrounding a desired event, will help the energy towards propelling itself to manifesting that which you desire. Beliefs are so important to acquiring the reality you desire, but when you add positive emotions to your beliefs, the energy that surrounds them propels them towards manifestation.

So positive emotions strengthen the energy.

Yes. Make sure that you surround your desires with positive emotions, for this is energy that is charged positively and thus, will propel itself towards manifestation. If you were to attach thoughts of fear and possible negative outcomes, then this energy would also propel itself towards manifestation. The law of the Universe is quite simple, and the energy will always seek its own compatible force; therefore, it is important not to attach thoughts of fear to your desires.

Beliefs are powerful and are imbued with energy that will affect the outcome of that which you desire. Beliefs of success will propel the energy of success towards manifestation. Beliefs about failure, coupled with the emotions of despair that surround failure, will propel energy towards manifestation of failure. The thoughts and beliefs that you hold can seriously affect your lives, and they do affect your lives. Be aware of the energy that is created by your thought processes because they will always affect the outcome of any given situation.

Based on what you're saying, it seems like the logic behind creating your reality is really quite simple. Why does it seem so difficult at times?

Melanie: It is more simple than you realize. It is so difficult because your ego gets involved with all its fears and need for control.

And this is where meditation comes into play.

Yes. This is why meditation is so important. It helps to tame the ego so that your fears do not hinder you. When you are having thoughts of doubt and question, immediately replace them with thoughts that are positive and freeing, for they truly will free you and propel you forward in your life.

Em: You are on your way to making significant changes in your life. As your new beliefs become engrained in you, there will be a confidence in your soul that makes you propel yourself forward with the same confidence. Make sure that you practice this method, for at times you may find yourself falling back into old patterns. The more you practice this, the firmer your new set of beliefs will become.

Melanie: Make your meditation a serious practice, for it truly works miracles as you would call them, and these miracles will astound you. Always remember to replace unwanted thoughts with thoughts that would bring abundance into your life. Laughter is also beneficial, and it will bring good health to you. Find many things to laugh about, and your mood will change from bad to good. When you have reached the levity level that laughter brings, then apply this feeling to beliefs that you want to create and situations that you want to attract, and you will notice quite a change in your life. It will take your life in a new direction.

Be patient with your belief exercises, for the time on your level may seem long. Some manifestations take longer time than others, but they will occur in its good time.

When you begin to adopt a new belief, you will begin to notice energy shifts within your body as you begin to assume the validity of these new beliefs. You will begin to notice changes almost immediately. Many of these changes are internal shifts, and you will notice them as a change of mood or feeling, internally. Be aware of the shifts inside of you, for they will seem very subtle at first, but then they will become deeper and stronger. This shift is a reflection of the positive shift of energy that is occurring. It is felt as a happiness within your soul or a spring in your step. This is the positive embrace that is felt as you shed a limiting belief and acquire a new sense of understanding. Continue to meditate on your new beliefs, and believe it is coming to you.

Demna: Make this time your special time, and you will be grateful to yourself; and be patient. We want to impress patience, for many of you want it all now. Make sure that you go into the belief exercises with the belief that this will work, and it will.

How does this process work? What is happening on a quantum level, and why is visualization so important?

Melanie: Your thoughts have energy. All that exists is energy, and energy attracts energy. If you visualize that which you desire, the energy is transposing the visual onto the interconnected graph per se, and allowing it to begin to occur through energy. If you break down the minutest organism, the minutest cell; if you strip that all away, you are left with the pure energy that is housed and operates the tiniest molecule. It is all illusion, and the clothing of organism is what covers energy.

By the interconnected graph, we refer to the threads of energy that we are all interconnected through. This graph is an energy field that encompasses us all, as well as all probabilities that exist. When we are visualizing a desired event, we attach certain emotions to this event. These emotions are imbued with energy, for all is energy. This energy attaches to the desired event which already exists as a probability within this interconnected graph or grid. This energy then propels itself into existence through the mutual energetic connection. All That Is contains all that is, and this includes all that is desired. We have only to visualize, and believe, and activate for these events to propel themselves into your life.

Every event that occurs within your life is in existence because you attracted and created it, whether consciously or not. It is, therefore, important to examine all your thoughts because they are more powerful than you realize. These thoughts create your reality, and then many of you wonder why these things are always happening to you. Well, quite simply, you create your reality through your thoughts and beliefs, and then you dwell within that which you created. If you want to change your life, then begin to examine your beliefs and thoughts, and you will see their correlation in your experience.

When you speak of the interconnected graph, are you referring to the grid that you described earlier?

Yes. This graph is a metaphor that we use to explain the concept. By graph, we mean the threads of conscious energy that we live in. Think of this conscious energy of the Source as an everlasting ocean, and we are the droplets of water that reside in this ocean and yet are a blended part of this ocean. By threads of conscious energy that we live in, we refer to the levels of dimensions that we occupy. Your dimension is but a thread of conscious energy. Our dimension is also a thread of conscious energy. Another way to explain this is by substituting the word planes for threads. Think of it as different planes of reality.

We spoke of pure energy, and on a quantum level, when you delve into the tiniest particle that exists, you will reach the energy levels that power all that exists. Strip your body to its tiniest elements, and strip these further to their tiniest levels. When all organic materials break down to the tiniest particle that exists, you will discover the energy behind it all. You will have stripped these elements right down to the conscious energy of the Divine Source. This conscious Divine Source is the Source that birthed the Universe and all it contains. This is the conscious energy that created you and powers you through your divine connection with each other. This is more than a connection in the way you would define it, for this connection is more of a merging of mutual energies, for without the Source nothing would exist.

Make yourself aware that the divinity of the Source is also your divinity, for you are merged as one with Source and All That Is. Your molecules house this energy, and you are powered more than you realize through the Source. This Source makes loving creation its purpose for self-actualization. You and your cells are comprised of this energy, as well as everything that exists. This is why we say that when you peel away all matter right down to the smallest molecule, you are left with the Source.

You say that it is all illusion. How can this be?

We, as spirit, create the world that we dwell in when we inhabit three dimensional form. We speak of the cooperative world that we create through our cooperative engagement with each other. The energy creates the world that we inhabit, and the matter that coalesces becomes real to our three dimensional senses. Beneath it all, lies the energy of spirit, and stripped of all the material clothing of our cooperative effort, this spirit is revealed. Mass is nothing but molecules that are floating together in the illusion that creates this mass. Mass is not as solid as you think. On a microscopic level, mass is not solid, but it is a sea of moving molecules. It is our cooperative belief that creates this illusion of mass.

Your scientists have discovered this illusion, for material mass is composed of atoms, molecules, and cellular structure that move and spin within material space. This moving mass of molecules then composes the many organisms and objects that exist. Through your three dimensional level of vibrational mass, you perceive them as dense solid material. This is due to the dense vibrations of your reality. You are a part of a cooperative consciousness that has agreed upon certain rules of engagement within your three dimensional level. Your senses perceive the solid mass due to the lower vibrations and compacted mass of your inhabited world.

How does this energy materialize? How does it become manifested?

Magnetism is the energy we speak of, and this magnetism powers everything; including your thoughts. When we speak of thoughts having energy, we mean this quite literally. It is true. Thoughts attract like minded events. The Universe operates on this level. It is how the Source operates. Do you notice how negative events always seem to happen to negative minded people? This is why, and if these people would shift the energy of their thoughts from negative to positive, then their lives will begin to change. This is how to utilize visualization in your meditation. Begin to project the visualization of that which you desire, and project the feelings and beliefs that you would surround yourself with. We will further explain this in our chapters to come.

Demna: Belief is powerful. As you continue your meditations, start to make room in your life for the changes that are to occur. They will be propelled to you by the Universe in many subtle ways. There will be occurrences that will bring your changes to you. Perhaps, meeting the people you need to meet or situations you need to happen. The Universe will set up a chain of events that bring these changes into your life. Some might call this synchronicity. The synchronicity factor is a tool per se, of the Universal Source, and many have witnessed it in their lives.

How does the Universe propel these changes to you? Is there a universal law in effect?

Melanie: Yes, there is a universal law, per se. The Universe, or the Source, is conscious energy of which we all are a part. Our energy is connected to the Source, and as such, we operate on the same principles as the Source; therefore, what we desire, we create through magnetism or the law of attraction which we will talk about in another chapter in this book. The Source, through our energies combined, creates reality, and our desires become reality based on our thoughts, beliefs, and emotions. As such, there will be events set in motion that will help propel our desired beliefs and thoughts into existence. Coincidences occur.

People who we need to meet come into our lives. How is this so, you ask? All is infused with energy, and the people who you need to meet align their energies with yours, and the events propel themselves into manifestation. Think of this mutual energy as two tuning forks that vibrate on the same note. This frequency is the same, and therefore, it is attracted to your frequency. Remember when we said that negative things always seem to happen to negative people? Their frequencies are the same. Their, so called, tuning forks are vibrating on the same note, and therefore, attracted to each other. Remember, birds of a feather flock together. Change this saying to frequencies of the same note flock together. It is so simple as to be astounding to you.

It really is! I'm just thinking that right now. This is so simple! So, if I understand this correctly, all you have to do is be aware of your thoughts, be aware of the emotions behind your thoughts, and if you choose wisely, according to the reality you want to create, you truly can manipulate reality.

Yes, yes. It is that simple, and it is the future of mankind's heritage to achieve his best life possible.

Can you summarize all of this for us in key steps? If you were to place them in order, what are the steps to manifesting your desires?

Identify your beliefs; especially your limiting beliefs.
Identify that which you desire.
Change your beliefs accordingly.
Attach the thoughts and emotions that are in tune with your new beliefs.
Visualize, and utilize meditation to set the stage for change. But you must truly believe your new set of beliefs, so meditate on them and allow yourself to embrace their truth.

Be aware of the events that start to enter your life, and seize them.

Be aware and open to the people who will begin to connect with you. Nothing is random. The Source, the Universe is orderly.

Demna: Keep your mind open to receive as the Source works through you. Meditation is your connection to the Source, and your mind is your vehicle to the Source. Keep your mind in tune with the Source and be aware of its internal guidance, for many changes can be directed through this connection, and your instincts per se, are guidance received from this Source. Be aware and be connected, and your path will be clear. God is the Universal Source and we can connect to him; God, being your term of usage. Many of you have different terms of usage, but it is all the same.

Love is God, is Universal Source, is All That Is. Your terms for the God Source may differ, but the meaning is the same. Be aware of this Source, and listen to its guidance. The stillness you feel in the meditative state is your access during this period of time. Always be sure to be open to receive.

Melanie: This is the end of our chapter. Anything else would be repetitive.

Chapter Three:

The Source

Melanie: In the chapter on meditation, we spoke about the stillness of the here and now and of the presence felt in this stillness. The Source, the Universal Source, is that which we spoke of. This Source is the Source energy that we are all connected to. It is conscious energy that has an awareness and consciousness. Whether you know it or not, you are continually accessing the Source's energy. Make no mistake about it; your energy is derived from the Source. Think of it as each person having an invisible umbilical cord that is connected to the Source. Just as an unborn baby is dependent on the mother's energy and sustenance through its umbilical cord, you are dependent on the Source's energy through your seemingly invisible connection to your Source.

You stated that the Source is conscious energy. This doesn't fit the description that most people have of God. I think that many people tend to personify God and see him as this biblical version of an old man with a white beard.

That is because you see yourselves as separate from God. You are not separate from God, but you are all extensions of God. There is no division other than the division that you create in your mind.

Then I guess my next question would be what is God?

God is the sum of all its parts. Think of God as the cloud in the sky that all of the rain droplets belong to. There is not really a separation because these droplets are sent forth from their Source, and when they evaporate, they become clouds once more. It is all relative. We are all a part of God, and when we set forth to inhabit Earth, we only separated as far as our unique individual identities are concerned, but we are still all a part of the mass consciousness of All That Is.

When we experience a physical death and transition to the other side, do we then reunite as one with God?

Yes, in a manner of speaking. You do, in so far as, whereby you re-merge with the collective consciousness of God, but you still retain all the identities you have ever had throughout all of your reincarnations.

We will attempt to explain this Source, using your vocabulary, but in truth, your vocabulary lacks the words and depth to fully convey the Source and its explanation.

Your Source has always been. It has no beginning or end, but exists in the everlasting now which also has no beginning or ending. It simply is, and it is all knowing, all aware, all powerful.

I'd like to stop you here because I'm having some trouble following this concept of God having no beginning. How can the Source have no beginning? Doesn't everything have to start somewhere, at some point in time?

No. Only in your three dimensional linear reality is there a beginning and ending. In the concept of time, it only exists as an illusion. We have always existed, but we are simply evolving as the Source continues its self-actualization. This is why your Universe is expanding, and contrary to your belief system, the Universe will not shrink.

It will not implode? It will forever expand?

Yes, because the experiences of the Source, in its quest for self-actualization through you as its Source souls, are expanding. As more worlds and realities are created, they occupy more space which, in turn, causes the current space to expand. Your Universe continues to expand as reality continues to expand, and reality contains a greater picture than you are aware of.

Your astronomers have had the opportunity to observe the birth of galaxies through their high powered telescopes. These galaxies are a part of the greater equation, and their birth and subsequent expansion is a small portion of your Universe. Your reality continues to expand as more probabilities are birthed, and these probabilities are quite real in their own Universe. You are creating worlds that you are not even aware of consciously, for many probabilities are spinning forth from your actions and thoughts. We will delve into this concept further in a chapter on alternate realities. Your Universe will continue to expand as long as the Source continues to exist. Your Source is eternal.

You've mentioned self-actualization a couple of times here. Can you explain to us, what self-actualization is?

Self-actualization is the Source's attempt, through journeying throughout many levels of awareness, to understand all of what it is. In journeying through many levels of reality, through its Source souls, the Source expanding all of what it is and creating greater and better parts of what it is. Through this journey, the Source has gained a greater awareness of itself and all that it is capable of.

When the Source existed as a singularity, it desired to learn all that it could contain. The Source longed to expand its reality and consciousness in an effort to know itself. It also longed to multiply itself as a parent longs to procreate. This led to the explosion of your Universe and the creation of all possibilities and probabilities that could be birthed into existence. This is the journey of the Source to self-discovery, through creation of all that it can become. This journey has become your journey as you represent the microcosm of this Source. We love you as the Source loves you, for we too are a part of this creative journey born through unconditional love.

Mankind is a great experiment for the Source, for it has allowed mankind to be co-creators, and this is the greatest gift to you. Mankind has been a great vehicle for the Source's journey in understanding, awareness, and creation.

This Source is a creative Source, and its thoughts become instant things of a concrete nature as we experience it, and depending on the laws of each separate plane, these thoughts take form as expected by their laws. For instance, your plane is three dimensional; therefore, these thoughts become realized as per this dimension. On a two dimensional plane, these thoughts would take form as per two dimensional laws and so forth as each dimension requires.

If the Source is the Creator, and its energy is creative, does this mean that we too are creators?

That's exactly it. You are separating yourself from the Source when you see it as an ultimate Creator and not include yourself in that equation.

If we are also creators, how can our thoughts become instant things in our plane when it takes us time to materialize the things that we want?

Because they don't become instant in your plane. Remember, we said as per the laws of each dimension. They become instant in the everlasting now, but due to the laws of your reality, you have to contend with linear time. Linear time dictates a beginning, a middle, and an end; therefore, birth, life, and death. Because you are connected to the Source, your thoughts become things also, but in your dimension there is the factor of time which is perceived in a linear fashion.

Many of us have realized our dreams and desires in good time, but many have not, due to the nature of these thoughts and the fears that have surrounded them. Make each desire you have an experiment in materialization, and you will begin to grasp all of that which we speak of.

The Source always is with us and connected to us. We are never apart from this energy because, theoretically, to be separated from this Source would mean that we would simply cease to exist in any form or matter. Even those who have lost their way are still connected to the Source, but they are simply lost and have not yet found their truth.

You believe many things regarding your creation. Know that as a part of this Source, you have a cooperative part in the creation of your world and reality; therefore, when we say that your thoughts become things, it is a literal translation.

How do we have a cooperative part in the creation of our world and reality?

Make no mistake about it. You and the Source are one; therefore, there is no alternative than being partners with the Source. The Source, in its quest for self-actualization, sent forth Source souls that are a part of, and connection of, the Source. Everything you do, think, or create, is accomplished with the energy of the Source because this energy is also your energy. Meditation will make this clear to you, for as you become more proficient in meditation, you will realize and feel this connection.

Demna: We would like to clarify the Source in a simple way, but in order to put it simply we must go into lengthy explanations.

You had an active role in the creation of this planet and Universe before you decided to inhabit it as human beings. You existed in the ether of creation while this Earth prepared itself for your readiness.

I don't mean to stop you here, but I have a few questions regarding who and what we were before we originally came to inhabit Earth. For starters, did we still have our individuality before we came to Earth as humans? What were we before coming to Earth as humans?

Melanie: Mass creation happened at once, and before you began your quest as a Source soul, you existed in the conscious energy of All That Is. Your individuality was birthed just as a baby is birthed before becoming a separate entity from its mother. You had an awareness that was merged with, and a part of the wholeness that is God, or the Source, as we term it. When birthed, you became a Source soul, but still a part of the Source. You were given a separate identity within the Source and free will which allowed you the freedom of expression in all its variables as a function of the Source's self-actualization.

When you speak of us being birthed, are you referring to our physical life birth, or pre-physical life?

Pre-physical. Before you became a Source soul, you were merged with God. Make sure you understand that being a Source soul does not separate you from God, but gives you consciousness within God.

And what is the ether of creation?

The ether of creation is that level of God, or Source, that birthed your Source souls. It is All That Is, and it is a level of pre-consciousness. Matter has a consciousness of its own in your three dimensional world, and the ether is the level of whence you came, and you do not remember this level as you occupy your current world. It would cause too much bleed through between our two realities, and you would have a difficult time reconciling the two levels. We exist in the ether of whence you came.

By pre-consciousness, are you are referring to our level of consciousness before we entered the three dimensional world?

Yes.

Demna: The creation of this planet began in the gasses of the physical Universe and believe us, NOTHING ABOUT EVOLUTION IS RANDOM. In capitals.

Nothing about evolution is random?

Melanie: Yes. It is planned. Everything is planned. Your free will brings into reality the events that you dwell on. When these events begin to propel themselves towards materialization, you will notice coincidences and synchronous events that might seem random, but actually, they are not. They are all planned events on another level that are propelled by the laws of magnetism; and we will delve further into this in a future chapter.

Demna: It must be emphasized that this creation was a planned event, and that when the planet was ready, you commenced to populate it as humans. You had a hand in this creation, for you are the Source, and you are part of the Source. There is no division between you and the Source other than the division you perceive in your mind. The Source does not have a separate mind than we all do; and that includes us, you, and all of existence, for we all dwell within the mind of the Source, and we all are composed of the Source. Meditation will make this clear to you.

As the Earth prepared itself for you, it went through a number of evolutions, from gaseous substances to solid mass; as these gasses fell in upon themselves and attracted mass, thus becoming mass. This is the Source creating a world to have a level of experience upon. You decided to experience the reality of this Earth and Universe to learn lessons and gain greater knowledge through awareness.

Are you saying that the Source created Earth so that we could experience physical life? Why would we need, or want, to experience physical life? If the Source is All That Is, then doesn't all physical experience already exist within the Source?

Melanie: No. In the beginning, as you would term it, there was nothing but the massive consciousness of God, or the Source, as we term it. Technically, your bible is correct in this matter. The Source wanted to understand more than what it was; and it was self-conscious, loving energy. Through love of itself, and in itself, it wanted to expand its awareness of itself and to encompass all possibilities of awareness; therefore, all planes and worlds burst forth from the Source.

I'm a bit confused by this. If time is an illusion, do all probabilities already exist, and if they do, wouldn't the Source have access to the experience of them all?

Make yourself not too confused. Time is an illusion, but that does not mean that nothing new can be created, for as new experience is felt and new realities are created, probabilities continue to expand.

And, new events will create new probabilities?

Yes, it is all growing. That is why we tell you that your Universe will never shrink. Many probabilities are being burst as you sit here.

So All That Is, is really all that currently is.

Yes, and All That Is will never shrink, or die, or cease to love you. We are so fortunate to exist, and the power of ultimate unconditional love ensures this. It ensures our continuation in perpetuity. You are here now and forever, in whatever form you will transform yourself into.

If I sit with this for a while, I can begin to make sense of this as it relates to human souls, but how do animals fit into all of this? What role do they play?

The Source, in its quest for self-actualization, wanted to experience all that it could, and animals will be discussed in our chapter on reality.

Demna: Make sure to absorb the truth of this chapter.

Em: As the Earth developed its readiness for you, it went through phases that you have documented history of. These phases are part of its natural evolution. An example of this is the dinosaur age. This era was not random, but it too was a planned event. Remember that all life has a soul, as you would define it, and all souls are part of the Source, which can also be defined as an energy source, and all souls are comprised of this energy source. You too, are energy source. Love is the Source, and it is from the Source of love energy that all thoughts and creation spring forth. Love Source is that from which all of reality, as you know it, springs forth.

You have existed on this Earth plane before, and many of the others in your life have existed with you. You have encountered many reincarnation journeys together for the purpose of life lessons and greater knowledge through mutual experiences.

You are now wondering about the reincarnation experience. Why would you think that you would simply cease to exist once you go through a physical death? If you are energy, then you cannot be eliminated. You can be transformed into another form, and then when you decide to enter the Earth plane again, you are simply transformed once more into the physical body, and on it goes. Your energy is eternal, for the Source energy is eternal and you are a part of this Source.

There are many people that have difficulty believing the whole reincarnation concept. Many of us believe that once we die, our souls move on to the afterlife and that's where we live out the rest of our spiritual existence.

Melanie: How dull.

Funny, I never considered it that way.

Your minds are limiting you when you believe these concepts. If the soul is on a quest for self-actualization and learning, then this concept defeats its purpose. When you reincarnate, you are expanding your experiences and learning opportunities. You are on a quest with the Source for self-actualization and learning. To only have one life and to then retire to the forever afterlife that you envision, is quite limiting and does not make sense in the greater plan of the Source.

Always be aware of your Source, for this Source will guide you through your reincarnations here on this plane. You will never die. YOU WILL ALWAYS BE SOURCE. In capitals.

Your energy is the power that runs your body, and your body is the vehicle that your Source dwells in while in that lifetime, just as you would dwell in, and operate, your car when you are driving it. When you step out of your car you do not die, but you simply move to another place. When your soul leaves your body, it too, simply moves to another place. The Source never dies. Think of yourself as a drop of water that simply returns to its ocean; the ocean being the Source, and the drop of water being the extension of its Source. In this manner, we experience other realities, and because we are connected to the Source, it too, shares directly in our experiences. God is our Source.

Make a list of the experiences you would like to have in your lifetime. Just as with the belief exercises, this list can be transformed into your reality here on the Earth plane. Meditate on these experiences and visualize them into existence. What would you like to experience? What would you like to learn? You have the ability, through your connection to the Source, to have this materialize. In due time, you will notice events shaping themselves towards the materialization of these desires. Make sure that your desires are not intended to bring harm unto yourself or others, but focus on good and positive results for all concerned. Make your list as long and detailed as you would like.

Demna: Be focused on goodness and love, for these elements have an energy of their own, and do not dwell on negative results, for they bring illness and negative results. Use visualization only for positive results, and bring only thoughts of love and goodness with you and you will receive such unto yourself. The Source is a loving energy and a conscious energy. Be aware of this, always. There is no place for hatred within the Source. God is good. God is love.

This is all very fascinating and leads us to so many more questions of who, and what God is. For instance, whom are we praying to when we pray to God?

Melanie: You are technically praying to your Higher Self and All That Is. The Source, technically, is your Higher Self because it is the conscious energy that birthed you, of which you are a part. By Higher Self, we refer to that part of you that is Source. When thinking of the concept of your connection to Source, visualize an ice berg. The tip of this ice berg is you, and the submerged part is that greater part of you that resides in the waters of spirit. This large part of you is the Source and all that it encompasses, including yourself. You are not separate from the Source, but your senses are programmed to perceive this sense of separateness in order to function within your reality. The Source is a great pool of conscious, loving energy of which you are a part; therefore, when you pray to God, you pray to that Higher Self which contains you.

Does God respond to our prayers?

Yes. God, and all your guides and angels, respond to your prayers. Your desires and dreams are prayers. With regards to your prayers, sometimes it appears that they are not answered because there is a higher purpose operating within your life. There is always a higher purpose at work. You might pray to be cured of a disease, but that disease might have been premeditated before you arrived on this planet; therefore, you perceive that God is not hearing your prayer.

Premeditated? What about people who are born into extreme poverty? Could this also have been premeditated?

This is all preplanned by those souls who are involved in that reality, and it is for the purpose of learning and teaching lessons to other souls.

Why would anyone choose to have such a horrible experience as a way of learning or teaching a lesson? Isn't there an easier way to experience the same lesson?

Make no mistake about it. It seems horrible, but it offers the souls a valuable lesson. It teaches about love for one another. Sometimes the best lessons in love are learned through suffering.

The journey of the Source soul is to achieve self-actualization and lessons in growth for the souls involved. These lessons are experienced by the whole, whether directly or indirectly. If all life was to be lived in an essence of perfect serenity and bliss, then the experience and growth would be limited to a narrow band of perception. There would be little room for the kind of growth you currently experience, for such a life lived would also be limited. The experience of self-actualization encompasses all possibilities, and lessons that are challenging are learned deeply and remembered for centuries, but lessons that are learned blissfully are forgotten soon as the soul embarks on a journey in search of the next blissful experience. It is like chasing a drug that never fully quenches your thirst or satisfies your life. Lessons that are challenging will teach you much more.

Many times have you been on this plane, but realize that this is not the only plane that you have experienced. Many of you have experienced other dimensions of reality, per se. The dimension you return to upon physical death is termed the Source. This is experienced as the white light that you connect with upon a physical death. There are many planes of existence and other planets in your plane that have life forms. Some of these have been inhabited by you in other life times of reincarnated experience.

You mention other dimensions of reality. What are these other dimensions of reality?

There are other planets, there are other planes that are planes of learning without the solid form of bodies, and there are levels of reality that are strictly cerebral within the expression of the Source.

So, when we reincarnate, we are not limited to reincarnating to this planet?

No, not at all. You have had reincarnations on other planets, and some of the alien life that is visiting you, are from planets that you have inhabited. Your experience is not only limited to this Earth, for the mind of our Source is vast and unlimited. You have had many types of experiences within the mind of the Source; and yes, even Earth experience dwells within the mind of the Source. Meditate on this concept, and you will experience an opening within your own mind. You have a mind that is as limitless as that of the Source, for you are connected to the Source, and therefore, you are the Source.

Then you would be confirming that alien life does exist on other planets.

Yes, absolutely. Why would the Source limit its experience to one lonely planet in one lonely Universe? It does not fit with the explanation and level of expansion that the Source wants to experience. Life lived only in this world of yours, singularly lived alone in this Universe, would be reason enough for implosion.

Why is that?

Because you are but a tiny dot in this expansion of All That Is.

Then this would mean that the Source is also the Source of all these realities.

Yes. Mankind is but a small part of the greater picture.

This will be a real eye opener for some people. Many people truly believe that we are the one and only life form in existence. If there exist many more life forms, it makes me wonder about the existence of God. Is there only one Source? Does God have a creator?
(At this point, there was a noticeable change in the energy that was coming through to us. It felt much slower and heavier, and we could tell that a new entity had joined us. We are always a bit nervous when a new spirit form comes through, but we felt that we were being protected by our guides and decided to continue with the session.)
Who is this?

We are Source.

What does that mean? Who are you?

You have called for knowledge that is of the outer and greater experience. Love is the ultimate God, and in Love all exists, and all that exists is so expansive that it seems to be incomprehensible in your terms. There is energy within energy, and it is all connected and contained within the greatness of the Ultimate Love Energy. It is all one, and to think that God has a God, is to imply separation. There is no separation. What you ask is this; is there a greater Source that gave birth to your Source? Think of God as greater than the mother ship of all creation.

Then, it is my understanding that the Source created other Sources. Am I correct in thinking this?

Just as you create, so does all conscious energy create. This is a concept that your consciousness, on your planet, does not comprehend due to limitations of beliefs, and time, and its laws of reality.

I really do want to try to comprehend all of this. Is there some way to break it down for us in simpler terms?

If you say that there is a God of God, then where does it end?

It doesn't end. It is infinite. It goes on forever.

Yes. Exactly. Spheres of conscious, loving, self-aware spheres within greater graduations of themselves.

This makes me think of those Russian dolls that fit one into the other. Layers upon layers.

Yes.

So, each layer is God, but they are all the same. They are all connected.

Yes, and just as there is no separation between you and the Source, there is no separation between each Source conglomerate. It is truly infinite. It is beyond the limitations of your thoughts and mind.

When we cross over, will we understand it all?

Yes, you will continue your learning, and there are many guides and teachers.

Is there any way to understand all of it while we are experiencing our physical life?

No. This is but a segment of the Source's experience. Just like life on another planet is just a segment. It is understood in segments through each journey of knowledge and experience.

If God is all that is and God is love, then how is it that hatred exists?

Make no mistake about it. It all exists within God. Hatred imparts experience and knowledge, just as love does. You are getting ahead of yourself. Save it for the chapter on emotions.

Meditate.

Chapter Four:

Healing

Melanie: Your energy is connected to the Source as you are connected to your breath. It is a part of you that has no separation, but you feel disconnected from it due to your perception of disconnection. It is you who feel disconnected as a result of your thoughts and beliefs. Your connection to the Source is quite real, and through meditation you will begin to perceive your connection to the Source. This connection is a direct conduit and can be utilized for many purposes, and the purpose described in this chapter is healing.

Em: As mankind evolves he will discover his divinity, and through this discovery he will realize that his divinity is a result of his direct connection to the Source. He will realize that through this connection to his Source he can access direct healing abilities that are generated by his thoughts, beliefs, and new found connection. You are able to access this energy, but it will require meditation and continued efforts at altering your belief system and expanding your awareness of mankind's capabilities.

Melanie: The Source is a source of energy that can be channeled through you and onto others because you are connected to the Source; therefore, you are a conduit of the Source.

Before we understand healing, we must understand illness and its origin. Many times have you heard that disease is dis-ease. That is, the soul being in a state of dis-ease. When you are not centered within your Source, it brings about a state of unease which is also dis-ease. This is where many of our illnesses and diseases originate. When your soul experiences constant upheaval with no release or comfort, it begins to fester within your organic body and many diseases can result.

What are the origins of our illnesses? What can cause them?

Mental conditioning and states of mind can cause illnesses. Your thoughts affect your body because all is energy, and it all interacts with each other. Some illnesses are caused by unresolved issues that are submerged without remedy. These issues fester like a boil that grows and eventually bursts. Such is illness. If some issues would be scrutinized, analyzed, and resolved, then the illness brought on by the issues would cure itself. Some illnesses are contracted by the soul before birth as part of the soul's learning journey. Some of these are assumed to teach lessons to others.

These illnesses may be to teach the parent a greater lesson in love, and they are not necessarily terminal. Many times these illnesses are corrected by medical professionals, and sometimes these illnesses are contracted for the lifetime of the soul. Many people carry anger, hurt, or negative beliefs throughout their lives. These negative emotions can begin to manifest themselves as illnesses within the organic body. Make yourselves understand that your journey here is for the purpose of spiritual growth, and such growth entails many lessons through many situations.

I recently heard some news about a local personality, who lives an extremely healthy lifestyle and follows a vegan diet, contracting breast cancer. How do you explain someone this healthy contracting cancer?

She needs to resolve issues in her life that have nothing to do with healthy eating. Some people may be healthy in their lifestyles, but this does not mean that they won't become ill. They must look into their souls and address unresolved issues.

What can people do when they have issues that they are unaware of?

This is where analyzing your beliefs can help you to discover unresolved issues you may not realize you have. If it is difficult, then there are many professionals that can offer counsel and help an individual delve into their souls. Psychologists can be a useful avenue to help identify and resolve submerged issues.

I would think that negative emotions would be a good indicator to help point you in the right direction.

Yes. Determine what these negative emotions are attached to in your lives.

You spoke earlier, of our thoughts and beliefs resulting in material manifestations. You also say that our thoughts, beliefs, and emotions affect our health.

Yes, they do, and how they affect your lives is quite simple. Emotions carry energy attached to them, and this energy affects your organic bodies. Negative emotions have a negative impact on your bodies, right down to the cellular level. Every cell is affected by emotions and beliefs. Your thoughts are energized by the magnetism that flows throughout us all. This energy's flow is determined by the quality of your thoughts, and beliefs supporting these thoughts. It can be positive, or negative, or simply neutral. If you continue to generate negative thoughts, as well as negative emotions surrounding these thoughts, they can in time, affect your body quite negatively also, and in time, this can fester into illness and disease. Your organic body is susceptible to the quality of your thoughts, beliefs, and emotions, for it too is comprised of the same energy that powers these thoughts, beliefs, and emotions. It is only logical that over a period of time it will succumb to these negative influences by expressing illness.

I think of people who tend to maintain a calm demeanor in their lives and let negativity roll off of them and then the people who seem to be very reactive towards things. I imagine it would help to not be a reactive person.

Yes, it would help, but at the same time, people who maintain calm might be avoiding issues, and this can build up also. Many people who appear calm on the surface may be concealing a very angry or maladjusted psyche. These people are brewing on the inside, but are trying to maintain a calm façade. This is most unhealthy because it remains bottled up and unexpressed. It would be far healthier to release this energy from the mind and body, than to let it fester into illness.

How do you explain babies and children who have life threatening illnesses? How could their thoughts and beliefs have affected their health? They seem too young for this possibility.

Yes. These souls have made an arrangement to have an illness to help another soul in his or her learning journey. It could be that this child never intended to live out a full life, but came into the world to teach his or her parents a valuable lesson for their own growth and learning, making it a journey of growth and understanding for all who may have been affected by the child's illness.

There are many paths of learning and many methods that help to instill lessons and learning for the souls involved in any given situation. Meditation will help to clear any confusion you have, but remember that a lesson is best learned upon reflection and may not always make sense at the time that an event is occurring. You might believe that it is tragic that a child assumes an illness or life threatening disease in order to impart a lesson, but it would be more tragic if the lesson was missed altogether. Remember that the tragedy lies in your reality only, but not in the greater reality that exists. The greater consciousness understands the true purpose of each soul's journey, and lessons learned for these souls are cause for celebration on the other side. If the lesson would be wasted, then what purpose was there for such a soul who must reincarnate to learn the lesson again? Love is the ultimate calling, and love imparts many lessons through many forms and situations in your reality. A lesson acquired is not a tragedy if it is well assimilated. Tragedies occur when the soul refuses to grow back towards love and Source.

What about in the case of miscarriages?

Miscarriages also have their purposes, and sometimes a miscarriage occurs because there is a defect in the fetus.

Are there ways that we can prevent ourselves from acquiring serious illnesses such as cancer?

Meditation and positive living will help you in avoiding these serious illnesses. Analyze your thoughts and beliefs as we have said.

What do you mean by positive living?

Live well. Do not indulge in foods that are not real, such as artificial man made products, for they are altered and not compatible with your organic composition. Make sure that what you ingest is compatible with your body's organic composition.

Mankind has been given all that he requires for the maintenance and sustenance of his organic body. You have many times been creative with that which you have been given, and through this creativity, you have invented many cuisines and food products. These are mainly healthy, but there are many of your food products that we would urge you to eliminate because they are unhealthy and detrimental to the lifespan of your organic body. We would urge you to eliminate synthetic foods and foods that have been manipulated and stripped of their vitamins and nutrients. Some examples of these foods include white flour, white sugar, and such foods that would fall into these categories. Synthetic sweeteners also fall into these categories. If you adhere to natural organic products that the Source has provided for you, you will notice an improvement in your health and an extension in the longevity of your lives.

When it comes to the matter of diet, are you better off ingesting a plant based diet versus an animal based diet?

No, not necessarily. Fish is good for you. Unfortunately, your fish are being polluted. How often, in the distant past, have you come across diseased fish? Diseased fish are a by-product of mankind's diseased living, and treatment of his environment. Make your diet varied, and include as much healthy food as possible. Red meat should be eliminated. Make it a habit to include all the nutrients that your body requires.

There are those of us who no longer eat meat. Can we lead healthy lives while cutting out this source of protein?

Yes. Be sure to substitute other protein sources, and supplement your diet with the vitamins and minerals that this meat would have provided you with.

Going back again to thoughts and belief systems; if changing our beliefs and thoughts help to heal our illnesses, how exactly does this work?

When you alter your beliefs and emotions and affect the lesson that you are to learn, this affects the organic cellular level of your body and can affect a cure. Just as negative thoughts and emotions can cause illness, affirmative and positive change can reverse illness. There are many ways to avoid these ill states of the body and soul, and if you begin to practice these methods, you can maintain a healthy level of body and soul.

Meditation is by far the best way to ease and maintain your body and soul. Just as you use meditation to alter your belief systems and attract experiences into your life, meditation can also be used to bring forth a state of good health and to heal the body and soul.

When you are meditating, focus on the white light entering your body and flowing through every portion of it. Focus on white light entering through your breath and filling your lungs. As your breath fills your lungs, also focus on drawing the white light into your entire body. Visualize it filling every part of your body, and visualize it healing every part of you. As you exhale, visualize the badness in your body being exhaled as darkness exiting your body. Practice this visualization with every breath; light entering and healing your body and darkness exiting and taking impurities and illness with it. Practice this until all impurities have left your lungs and until you visualize white light entering and white light exiting. Always focus on good health as you do this meditation. Do not focus on ridding bad health, but attaining good health. Focusing on bad health will attract bad health. Focusing on good health will attract good health. Meditate every day. Make it a habit and it will become a natural part of your life. Make a list of the healthy habits you want to adopt, and make it a point to focus on these habits during the meditation process.

Healing can take place at any point in an illness' progression. It depends on a strong connection to the Source and a belief in the illness' ability to be cured. If the recipient does not take an open view of the process, it is almost impossible to affect the illness to heal. In other words, if the recipient does not believe in the possibility of being healed then he is not attracting good health.

You state that healing can take place at any point in an illness' progression. How can this happen? What should a person be doing to promote healing?

Meditate on changing your beliefs, emotions, and life for the better. Have a positive outlook, and utilize visualization as part of the healing process. If you can get to the root of what is affecting your life and resolve the issue, it can resolve the illness. Many times there have been spontaneous remissions and cures because the person made a great realization and achieved a great resolution in his life.

Healing Method

To affect a healing on another, you must first meditate and connect to the Source. Follow the method in chapter one on connecting with your Source. When you have reached the stillness of the now, focus on attracting healing energy towards you. Focus on opening a channel to the Source, and focus on drawing its energy through you and onto the recipient. It is not important which method to use to send energy to the recipient. It is only important that you use a method that works for you.

Some like to draw energy with an open palm facing upwards, and send the energy with an open palm towards the recipient. Others like to visualize energy entering through the head and leaving through both hands towards the recipient. Use the method that works for you or develop your own.

What kind of healing thoughts should you direct towards someone whom you are conducting a healing session on?

Loving thoughts and thoughts of good health and healing. It helps to send the appropriate energy to the person you are healing. It helps to visualize the illness dissipating within the patient, and it helps to visualize white light entering the affected area.

Is it also of benefit when people pray, either in groups or individually, for the affected person?

Yes. This is a powerful direction of healing and loving energy towards the afflicted person. Healing energy and prayers are powerful tools that we can use for healing. Prayers have energy just as thoughts do, but prayers are specifically focused and loving, and therefore, are connected to a more specific and loving energy. A prayer of love and healing helps to focus the Source energy on the recipient, thus assisting in the healing process.

Once you have meditated, it is important to ascertain where the illness is located within the body. Ask your patient for his feedback, and trust your senses to direct you to his illness. Have your recipient focus white light on his illness while you direct your healing energy and healing thoughts towards the location you are focusing on. If your patient is not present with you, then you can perform a long distance healing. It would help to have a photograph of the person in such an event. Meditate to make the Source connection, and follow the same steps as if the person was present.

God has given us many abilities through our Source connection. If we stay connected through the Source, then we can enjoy the fruits that this connection brings us.

Follow this method, and focus your energy and belief to affect a healthy and positive change. As you continue this practice, you will develop your own methods.

We do not advocate eliminating your medical methods and adopting healing energy methods only. You are still connected deeply to your physical beliefs on the Earth plane. We recommend healing energy as an addition to your practical medical methods.

What if you are taking medications? Should you suspend the use of medications while you are having a healing performed on you?

No. We do not advocate this because your belief systems are powerfully rooted in your medication of the western societies. Medications that are helpful can help heal a person who has powerful beliefs in the healing qualities of these medicines.

Medications of the western societies are largely obtained, originally, from organic compounds found in nature. These medications are transformed during the manufacturing process, and many are synthesized. Your early medicine men understood the healing nature of many plants and substances occurring naturally on the Earth. Your modern day medicine has many times improved on these remedies, but many times they have, with these improvements, caused many unhealthy side effects, and many times these side effects can be life threatening. Your beliefs in these medications are so deeply rooted that you will overlook the side effects in favor of being healed, as your beliefs dictate. It is because your beliefs in these medicines are so strong that we urge you not to discontinue their use during a healing session. At one time in mankind's history, belief in the medicine man's healing strategies were so strong that these too, facilitated healing at that time; so you see, belief plays an important role in the healing of one's body.

Are there exercises, such as yoga and tai chi, that deal with the alignment and flow of energy that are helpful?

Yes. These exercises deal with the proper alignment of energy within the body. Acupuncture is a method of aligning energy also. When energy is blocked within the body, it creates areas of blockage that in turn, create areas of illness in the body. By redirecting the flow of energy and releasing blockages within the body, you can begin to feel a better sense of health and energy within yourself. These methods, such as yoga and others that help to redirect and unblock energy, can help you to heal your body.

If you are performing a healing on a person, is it possible for you to take on that person's illness?

No, the person affecting a healing is driving out the bad energy or affliction. He is not assuming the affliction. In the process of driving it out, he is driving it or rather, directing it away. People who feel the blockages or pain that their patient has, are not assuming the illness, but are attuning themselves to the person who they are working on. Sometimes this can be confused by the healer or others, as a symptom of assuming the illness of the person being healed. This is not the case. No one can assume another's illness as a result of healing practices. These practices ensure that the healing energy is being assimilated by the patient while the blocked energy or illness is being directed away and out of the body.

The healing chapter does not need to be long and complicated, for this is a simple process. Live your life in health and in good thought.

End of chapter.

Healing

Chapter Five:

Intuition

Melanie: Many are guided by an inner sense of knowing and intuition. This is your radar, and it is a powerful source of guidance. When your soul is connected intuitively to the Source, it can begin to receive signals of guidance. These signals are perceived as an inner tug towards a certain direction or a certain answer to a question. By stilling your soul through meditation, you can begin to open these channels of communication and guidance.

Your senses were once open when you were a child, and you had many experiences and communications with the other side. As you grew and matured, you became more firmly rooted in the reality that you currently dwell in. As a child you still had one foot per se, in the other side, and there was very little division between the two sides because the rules and lines between these two realities were blurred. How could you be firmly rooted in this reality if you did not understand the rules?

Many of you had imaginary friends but realize now, that these friends were and still are quite real. They spoke to you in a manner that you understood, and they guided you through your childhood. They are still with you now. The only difference is that you have become rooted in a reality that does not acknowledge their existence, let alone their guidance. Meditation can open these channels again.

When you became rooted in the belief systems of this reality, you effectively shut out the friendships of your youth with the other side. By refusing to acknowledge our existence, you have closed the door that was once open to you. Meditation will help to reopen this door. Meditation will reconnect you with the Source and will help to unlock that which you locked a long time ago.

Who were these imaginary friends that we all had, and what was their connection to us?

Imaginary friends are your guides in life, and these guides are souls who have not reincarnated in this lifetime, but are in the other realm and are guiding you. Some of these guides are relatives who may have crossed over before your birth or early in your life. They may be a great grandparent or a great aunt. All these are possibilities.

Much has been said about spirit guides and intuition. Always remember that your intuition is your connection to the Source, and your spirit guides can help to guide your intuition because we too are connected to the Source, and through the Source we are connected to you, and together we are a part of the ocean of conscious energy. Meditation is the conduit that will reconnect us as we were once connected in your youth. You can make the reconnection easier than you think, and it is as simple as fifteen minutes of meditation a day.

You have always had the ability to connect with us, but have forgotten your Source as you rooted yourself in this reality. Make the time to meditate, and we will reconnect with you as you progress, and we will continue to guide you along the path you are on. We have always been with you, but your mind has been closed. Many times have we attempted to guide you, but you have had your eyes shut and have not heard us.

How does this all connect to intuition, you ask? We are the voices of your intuition, and we have tugged at your heart many times to direct you on a path that you should best undertake. Many of us have guided you through life by using your intuitive self as a compass for direction, and you have many times ignored our voices because your logical and analytical mind got in the way. Be aware of this, and be aware of your inner guidance because this is the true compass of your soul. Be aware in the stillness of your soul, for this is where you will hear our voices as we guide your direction in life.

How do we know that our intuition is guiding us and not our ego or logical mind?

You will know because in the depth of your soul it feels right. When it is your ego or logical mind taking over, there is a disconnect from your soul and mind. It won't have that quality of feeling right. The voice of ego is the chatter that goes on inside your head, while the voice of intuition is that part of you that speaks not in words, but in feelings. It is that part of you, deep inside, that senses on a feeling nature whether something feels right or feels wrong. Your ego is the voice that focuses on whether or not you are good enough or capable enough, whereas your intuition simply understands on a spiritual level which is the level of the Source connection.

Meditation has been a recurrent theme throughout the chapters. This is because meditation is the line of communication between the Source and your soul. It is through meditation that the connection is possible, and we will always be there to guide you and help you as best we can. Be aware of our presence in your life, and the doors will open for us to connect. We speak to you in many subtle ways such as a tug inside your heart to a certain direction or a physical appearance as a good Samaritan when you are in need. You see, the rules of your reality do not apply to us, and we can materialize in those times of need. With practice in meditation, you can open the doors between the invisible barrier that separates you from us because this separation can be dissolved through a shift in your reality, and we can once again be available to you as we were in your youth. Keep the practice of meditation up, and you will be able to open many doors.

How will we perceive our intuitive guides once we have dissolved this barrier through continued meditation?

You will feel a connectedness of energy and spirit. It is as if you are experiencing a vivid dream, but are awake mentally. In your mind, you will see us enter the picture, and we will display a sense of ourselves that we control. It is like experiencing a waking dream. We will interact with you and communicate with you, and you will know it because of the quality of realness. It is as if you are connected through your soul and energy.

Are you speaking of when we are in the meditative state?

Yes.

You mentioned appearing as a good Samaritan. Are you saying that you come to us, not only intuitively, but in some cases you may physically materialize as well?

Yes. We can do this and have done it on occasion. There are times in need, when a stranger will come to help you, and then when you look in our direction again, we are simply gone. You have heard of these situations when the helper disappears as suddenly as he appeared in the first place. You will not see us materialize or dematerialize, but when these events occur, know that it is your guide who has appeared to you.

Would a guide ever appear to us physically just to make a connection?

No and yes. Many times we appear in the safest and most unfearful way possible. There are times in great need when we have appeared to mankind, but these times are rare.

Trust your intuition even though there are times when your logical mind gets in the way. There is always a good reason why the soul has its own direction. Let it guide you to where you should go, and fear not the consequences. It is in those times that you have disregarded your intuition that the consequences have been undesirable, and remember that there is always something good waiting for you when you follow your inner guidance. Beware of ignoring your inner guidance. This is your God given compass and serves to guide you in the right direction in life. Meditate, and allow the answers to your questions to formulate in your heart.

What is our intuition?

Your intuition is the part of your soul that is the direct line of communication with the Source. You were given intuition as a guidance system for the purpose of guidance in your life. It is something that is unavoidable, for since you are of the Source, this is a natural part of the Source that lives inside each and every one of you. Just as a ship has radar, so do you have a system of checks and balances that serves as your radar. Logic controls the mind for calculations, but intuition acts as your radar or guidance system for the purpose of navigating through the spiritual course of your life. This spiritual course determines the lessons of the soul as it journeys through life, and your intuition helps to guide the soul while the mind has the logical capacity required for calculations. Intuition can be referred to as your sixth sense. It is the unspoken sense that you have. It is the feeling sense of connection that you have with the Source.

What is the difference between our intuition and psychic abilities; for example, abilities such as clairvoyance, clairaudience, and clairsentience?

You have answered your own question in a sense. The intuition is a subtle guidance system that everyone has, and some people have something called psychic abilities. These people have a deeper connection on a soul level, and they can sense and see things on a deeper level than most people. These psychics are more evolved than the average person. When we speak of mankind opening his third eye, this is what we mean. These people have an open third eye.

Can you explain what our third eye is?

It is what mankind refers to as the chakra that exists between the eyes of your brow. It is the third eye of psychic awareness and deep intuition. It is the part of mankind that connects him to spirit and allows him to communicate in a grander sense than his three dimensional sense. It is the means he has that allows him to see that which cannot be seen by his human eyes. It is his spiritual eye, and this spiritual eye operates in what you refer to as the sixth sense, but it is the fourth dimension and is the additional layer to your three dimensional world. As mankind opens this awareness within himself, he will become a more sentient being in the full sense of the word.

Can we all develop our intuition on a deeper level or a psychic level, such as these people?

Yes, it is possible, and some seekers spend an entire lifetime searching for this quest.

How would we develop this ability if we wanted to?

You are asking for knowledge that is rather simple. The desire to develop this ability will in, and of itself open the doors of intuition and spirit. There are no tests, for none are needed. There is the desire to open the third eye, which is followed by dedication through meditation, awareness, and spiritual connection on an internal level. Through practice, and dedication, and personal searching, the student will discover his way, for each journey is personal and depends on the willingness of the student. Be open; be aware; especially to the signs that the Source will send you. Everyone has the gift and ability latent within their souls, and it is a matter of seeking and discovering through each soul's private journey. Meditation is a good beginning. There are many avenues such as yoga and tai chi because these practices deal with running your internal energy. It is a quest of time, and practice, and deep connection with the Source.

Em: The methods we listed are a few good avenues. Meditation especially, but any method that connects you internally to your soul is appropriate. Different approaches work for different people. Some engage in chanting and some engage in rhythmic drumming also, but it is important for each soul to discover the methods that work best for him or her.

I've never heard that yoga or tai chi could be helpful in this way.

No and yes. It is not the true path, but it is a supplementary path. There are some who have this gift naturally, but to develop it fully can be a dedicated lifetime journey.

Em: We all have questions in our lives, and sometimes we can feel quite lost on our journeys. It is during these times that your intuition can help guide you through life's obstacles and stresses. By calming your inner self and stilling your soul, you can begin to ask and receive answers to your questions. Listen to your inner self, for the answers lie within, and the guidance that your intuition offers you will never steer you wrong. Always cast your doubts aside, for they are rooted in fear, and fear creates a foggy mind and a foggy path. Always meditate before hand to calm your soul and still the turmoil that lies within. Once you have reached a level of calmness, you can begin to sense the direction that your intuition would guide you in. We will always be there to help facilitate you and will keep you safe inside this process.

Melanie: Make time to meditate to clear the clutter from your mind, and this will help to keep you in tune for the guidance that your intuition gives. When you are centered in your soul, the signals are clearer, and you can have a better understanding of the direction your intuition is guiding you in. Meditation is a recurring theme, for it is the hub for all your inner senses. Have faith in the process, for it truly works, and you will benefit greatly through following your intuition. Make time for yourself because only you can guide your soul's ship, and every captain should be centered in his inner self.

Chapter Six:

Guides

Melanie: We spoke briefly of your guides and invisible friends in the last chapter. In this chapter we will elaborate on this further.

When you decided to journey to this plane, the decision was shared throughout the ocean of conscious energy, and there was a cooperative effort between you and the Source. Many guides also became involved with you in this effort, and it became a joint journey. You engaged the guidance of other souls to keep you on this path of limited consciousness. It is limited in relationship to the vast and intelligent consciousness of the communal Source.

Can you explain the details of how the decision of our journey to this plane is made?

Many of you have been here many times, and there are many lessons and experiences that you have undertaken before birthing into your current reality. We have also reincarnated into your Earth reality on many occasions. It is a very simple process from our point of view. It is a decision made by each Source soul, but this decision is shared among all of us who journey with you. Some Source souls agree to birth onto Earth to share the journey. These Source souls may become your relatives or friends along the journey and share knowledge, learning, and experiences along this journey. It is a group effort, and those of us who stay on this side, agree to be your guides throughout your journey.

The Source soul has free will, and at times, the decision involves nothing more than a desire to experience a particular culture or country on your planet. At other times, this decision can involve a soul's desire to learn a specific lesson or lessons, or it may be a desire to assist in another soul's spiritual journey. There are multitudes of reasons why each soul reincarnates, and there are many plans and communications that transpire as a result of these decisions as other souls join in to assist in each journey. Many of mankind's journeys have been for the purpose in assisting the Source's self-actualization plan, and this plan includes as its mandate, the evolution of mankind upon this planet, inclusive of all the individual evolutions that encompass this grand master plan. Mankind has much evolving to do.

Many of you on this planet have become unfocused because you have ventured off course due to the blindness of this reality that you dwell in.

Can you explain this statement? What do you mean by the blindness of this reality?

It is quite simple. Your reality is limited compared to the one you left to enter Earth. The Source soul does not remember, on a physical level, where he came from or what his decisions were before birthing into the Earth level. His soul remembers, but this is hidden from the three dimensional reality you occupy. Free will comes into play also, for although each Source soul comes here with a plan, the free will of mankind can always get in the way of his true calling. This is why meditation is so important. It helps the soul to center its self and connect to the Source of whence it came. Many of you have forgotten your soul's purpose, and it is important to re-center yourselves.

Why is this hidden from our three dimensional reality? What is the purpose?

The purpose is to focus on each lifetime without bleed through, as bleed through would interfere with the life at hand. There is no need to allow bleed through from all other lives, as this would cause much confusion and would not serve any purpose. Bleed through from other lifetimes and realities would be as many screens appearing at once. Much focus would be lost, and it would throw your world into mass confusion if there were not rules of engagement for the operation of this reality. Remembrance is also the remembrance of other realities whence you came from. If these decisions and where you come from is so easily remembered and known, then what purpose is served by learning a lesson you already know or are aware of?

Lessons, all are based on love. That is the ultimate lesson, and each journey reflects the lessons of that particular lifetime. It is important to have a fresh slate in each reincarnation, and by this we mean that each lifetime should be independent from any others. In this manner, all lessons are fresh and unique in each soul's present journey. Bleed throughs are counter productive at times because they offer a distraction that may throw the Source soul off his current path. In this manner, each lesson can be understood and focused on more fully.

Why did we need to engage the guidance of other souls to keep us on this path of limited consciousness?

Many of you, as we mentioned, have lost a sense of your spiritual sight due to the density of the plane you inhabit. It is because of this loss of spiritual sight that guides are engaged to help keep you centered in your Earthly journey. Guides are here, not only to keep you centered on your journey, but if utilized properly, there is much we can teach you, and the two of you (Tina & Tilde) are a prime example of this utilization. You are utilizing us to write this book, which not only enhances your journey on this plane, but also the journeys of those who read this book and engage the practice of meditation.

This is a good example of how Tina and I are able to utilize your guidance as teachers, but this example is very specific to the two of us. Many people's senses are not developed enough to channel information. What are some examples of ways in which they can further utilize your guidance?

Meditate to connect with the Source. In this connection, you will help to open your spiritual channels, and it will help you in listening to your intuitive self. Your intuition is a method that we can utilize to assist you, and this is why meditation is so important. By listening to your inner self, you can gain access to our communications as we connect with you on a soul level. Meditation is the most important tool at your disposal. It will open the channels of your soul to a greater communication with the Divine Source. Listen to your deepest sense of soul. This is why we tell you to listen to your intuition. It is our connection.

We joined with you at the beginning of your Earthly quest and waited for your birth day to arrive. We have been with you ever since that day and before that day. Many of you can remember having invisible friends as a child, and many of you have forgotten the invisible friends that you had. We played with you in your childhood, and we entertained you as well. You were never alone. We spoke to you as silently as we could through our souls. We did not communicate with you on a verbal level, although it may have seemed that way at the time. We spoke to each other in our own private language, and at times you communicated to us in your verbal language, for we were quite real to you, and you perceived us thusly, for you were not rooted in the laws of three dimensional reality. We were, and still are, very real. Your parents and elders thought you were engaging in child's play, but in reality it was real play. We have always been with you in this lifetime, and at times that you feel you are alone, you are actually surrounded by many of us, and in times of angst, we are trying to console and guide you through your experience.

Em: Always know that we have much faith in you, and we are here to guide you through your lifetime. We have spent many lifetimes together, and there have been times when you have been guides to us as we embarked on our physical journeys in our reincarnations. We have been together a long time, and we have much invested in your spiritual growth here on Earth.

Why would a soul choose to be a guide, rather than reincarnate?

Melanie: It is out of a sense of service to the reincarnating souls. There have been times when you have been guides to other souls on Earth. We are all connected through love and Source energy, and we are all devoted to each other and the Source. Love is the thread that connects us all, and through service to other souls, we are………..

(The energy suddenly shifted here, before this last sentence could be completed.)

Source: Love is ultimate, and our service to you is our expression of love. We love you so deeply that we would not want to lose a single soul to despair or uncertainty. Through our guidance, we hope to guide you all to achieve the best direction for your soul's discovery of Source actualization and love. We would guide you to your best potential, and it is out of pure love that we do this for all Source souls.

Em: When guides reincarnate, there are those who guide us. We have all been guides, and we have also reincarnated. It is.

As a guide, are you still evolving through the experiences of the person you are guiding?

Yes. We are all always evolving. It is due to our interconnectedness that we all learn and grow together. What is learned by one soul is assimilated by all souls through our interconnectedness. Meditation will make this clear to you. The Source encompasses all souls, and guides, and all of existence, and it is through the Source's quest for self-actualization that we have all been sent forth, therefore, all that is experienced by one is experienced by the whole. This is God's ultimate plan. Self-actualization.

Can you continue to evolve if you choose to remain a guide and not continue to reincarnate?

Yes, but it is not as you think it because we are learning and growing on this level in ways that are not directly connected to you. We learn through experiences and learning opportunities on this level that we dwell on, for we have teachers just as you have teachers on Earth. There are schools of thought and learning in our reality, and we continue to learn and grow without the use of a physical body or a three dimensional life. It is simply another plane of reality with its own set of rules of engagement that pertain to this level. It is simply another state of being. You must remember that Earth is not the only reality in existence, and it is but one level of learning and existence. Many discoveries that exist on Earth have been processed on our side first. This is but one example of the cooperation between our worlds. There are many of us who are working with those of you on Earth as teachers and guides, just as we are with Tina and Tilde. There are many of us who are helping to guide the development of your planet. There are many of us who are helping to guide the development of other planets and realities. The learning and growth opportunities are as limitless as the mind of the Source.

How can we continue to keep ourselves open to the presence of the Source and our guides while we are living our day to day lives outside of meditation?

Keep connected to your inner self, and listen to the gentle leanings of your soul. By meditating on a daily basis, you and many others will help to maintain the center that you strive for. It is through meditation that you will center yourselves.

Make sure you take the time to meditate, for this is the path to all areas of enlightenment while you journey on this Earthly path of yours. Make time to connect with yourself on a soul level, for it is at that level that your guides can connect with you. Always be aware that our presence is with you, and our purpose is to help guide and protect you. Many times you have not heeded our guidance because you have been disconnected from your inner self and have been blind to the information that is available to you. Be aware, for awareness is your radar scope, and it helps to open your self to our gentle proddings in the right and best direction for you. Be aware, for in this awareness we will make our presence known. Keep yourself open, and we will try to reconnect with you as we once did in your youth.

Melanie: We had many experiences with you throughout your childhood. We communicated with you, and at times, we showed ourselves to you when you needed our guidance and protection. There have been times when we have materialized during your youth and have kept you company while you made the progression into this reality, and there have been times many of you have seen us as friendly strangers in times of need. There have been times when we have warned you of impending danger. You may have heard a voice, only to turn and discover no one there. Your guides are always with you and want to help you in your journey through this lifetime.

Guides are around you for your guidance and service. Think of us as your co-pilots in life's journey. We are never far, and you have only to call upon us, and we will be there for you. When you need us, try to still your soul so that you may hear what we are trying to say to you. Our language is not verbal, but our language communicates to the feeling tones of your soul.

Be aware of the inner soul direction. Make sure that you are centered, and push aside your feelings of doubt and fear. When your soul is tranquil we can best communicate to you, and you are in a better space to receive and identify our gentle prodding. It will appear as if you get a feeling about a direction that you should take or a situation that you should avoid. It is a sense that something either feels right or it doesn't. These are our guidance efforts to give you a direction that you should take. Be comforted in knowing that your best interests are always in our hearts, and that we have a vested interest in your well being. Don't fear the process, but let the process take its natural course.

Be aware that if you do not follow your instincts, that then, there is always the possibility that you won't like the consequences, and that it may put you into situations that are not pleasant or even dangerous. Make sure that you are in tune with your soul and the decisions that you make. We can be here to guide you, but we cannot always save you from your bad decisions. Be aware, and be in tune. Some would call it following your gut feeling. This is what our guidance is, and we will always bring the right decision to you. We are always here; just call upon us, and your answers will come to you through your instincts.

In times of emotional upheaval and confusion, how can we navigate through the turmoil to reach that place where we can access our guides and their help?

Find even a moment where you can still your soul and connect to your guides. We will always answer you through your intuition. Just be centered and call on us.

I would think that the more a person meditates, the more balance they would achieve in their lives, leading to fewer moments of feelings of turmoil in their lives.

Yes. This is true. A person, who is not spiritually connected is prone to more episodes of confusion and many base emotions. Always remember that your guides love you and want to have a relationship with you. We have been with you since forever, and we will continue to be with you forever, for there truly is no beginning or end, but just an everlasting now. Be good to all that cross your path, for in life, there will be much opportunity for you to offer your guidance to others and for others to offer their guidance to you. Do not doubt yourself. We will be here to guide you, and may love be your beacon.

Be harmonious in all your decisions.

Guides

Chapter Seven:

Love

Em: You have a great capacity for love because you are a part of the Source, and the Source is love. Always be loving in your soul and towards others, for love is truly the glue that binds us all together.

In the beginning of this planet or reality, as you would term it, there existed the Source or God, as you would term it. Because the Source wanted to expand itself and experience itself through many dimensions and levels of experience, it began to experiment with creating other worlds and planes with which to have these experiences. It was through love of itself and its components that it sent forth souls to experience growth and love through its endeavors. God is pure unconditional love that many on this Earth have yet to experience.

It is through the separation with God and through our journeys on this plane that we are rediscovering love, and the many lessons and tribulations that we experience are for the purpose of discovering love in our lives. It is a journey of lessons for the discovery of love of ourselves and of others.

If we are a part of the Source and the Source is pure, unconditional love, then why are we on a journey to discover love of ourselves and others? Should this love not already be naturally present in all of us?

Melanie: When we speak of disconnection, we are speaking of the mental and spiritual disconnection as a result of forgetting who and what we are. Because we have forgotten this and because of free will, we must journey and repeat our physical lives to learn the lessons of love and to remember who we are and why we were sent forth in the first place. We have not this natural love when we reincarnate because of our lost sense of identity.

It is through loving others that we can love ourselves and through loving ourselves that we can love others. A mother gives birth and falls in love instantly with her child. It is through the journey of motherhood that the individual learns the lesson of unconditional love, for there is nothing that a mother would not do for her child.

I'm not sure I understand what you mean by disconnection or "through the separation with God."

When many of the Source souls were sent forth for the purpose of the Source's self-actualization, they became so attached to their dense bodies that they lost focus of their purpose and became spiritually separated from the Source. Since then, these souls have been on a reincarnational journey to find their way back to the Source and its love.

Em: Love is the lesson we are here to learn, and many of us must repeat our lives many times to learn this, to truly be reconnected again with the Source. You have had many opportunities in your journeys to learn the lesson of love, and there are times when you have failed, and there are times when you have loved and learned the lesson. History has many examples of love. Romeo and Juliet, Anthony and Cleopatra, for instance, but there are many examples of failed lessons. Hitler is the most recent example of such failure. These souls, in their separation and mistaken love of ego, have much to learn before reconnection with the Source, for the Source is love, both pure and unconditional. Make sure that in your journey on this Earth, you allow yourself the capacity to love yourself and others.

Why is there so much hate in the world? Why do some people carry so much hate within themselves?

Melanie: Because of this separation that we speak of. These souls have disconnected from their true Source and have forgotten their true spiritual identity.

How can we help these people to experience love and help them to eliminate the hatred that they carry?

We can teach through example, and we can teach love by loving these people unconditionally so that the hatred is washed away. Sometimes, hatred is a form of protection for these people, for to love is to risk and be hurt.

How do we unconditionally love people whom we dislike, or have angered us, or are complete strangers? How can we do this when we don't genuinely feel this love for these people?

Meditate, and in meditation, when you connect to the Source, remember that these people are also a part of this Source. Put yourself in their shoes and feel their sorrow, for in feeling their sorrow, you can begin to feel compassion for them. Remember that these people are your brothers and sisters, and just as you would feel anger towards a brother or sister, you also retain the love that allows you to forgive them. If you can see everyone as brethren, you can allow love to rise within you towards them. Remember that there may be people who would feel this dislike towards you as well. Would you not prefer them to love you instead, for truly we would all prefer to get along and live in true peace and harmony. Imagine what this world would be like if we all got along and truly gave love and peace a chance to flourish.

Are there any lessons to be learned in a soul's failed lesson in love?

Yes. It is through failure that we sometimes learn our greatest lessons, for in this failure comes the conviction to learn and not repeat the failure. We spoke of Hitler as being a failed lesson in love, but this lesson has also taught mankind much about love and compassion for our Source soul brothers and sisters. We must learn this lesson, for it should not ever need to be repeated again, and though many perished, we must feel love and compassion for those brave souls who undertook the journey to teach mankind the depth of this failed lesson in love. Meditate, and be in the Light of Love.

Love is the most powerful energy in the Universe. It has enough power to move heavy objects that one would think impossible to move. When a mother sees her child in distress, her love will blindly lift something as heavy as a car off of this child. Love so empowers and adrenalizes the body, as to make this possible. The power of love can heal illness and change the course of history. It can move a nation to change its course. Gandhi is a good example of this. He so loved his people and his nation that he affected its course. Do not underestimate the power of love, for it is truly a transformational energy, and it can transform your life. Love yourself as you would love your precious child, for you are someone's precious child and deserving of love.

How can the power of love heal illnesses?

Jesus healed through the power of love, for he so loved all of that which was his Source and all of that which was connected to his Source. He so understood the Source and his connection on a deep spiritual level, that he was able to directly access this power. When you are truly connected to the Source, your love and understanding will be so profound that you will be able to heal any illness by directly accessing this power.

Em: Meditate to connect yourself to the Source, and when you achieve the level of stillness, focus on drawing the Source's love energy to yourself. Invite it to fill your vessel and your soul. Feel it moving through you and washing over you. Extend this love energy to others, and visualize it washing over them. By sending love to others, you can affect a vibrational change within them. Remember that we are all connected to the Source, and we are, therefore, connected to each other. We are all brothers and sisters as you would term it; therefore, love each other as you would love the members of your family, and know that what you give, you will receive.

Be loving towards all of humanity as a whole. If we all practiced love on a daily basis, it would change the world in such a manner as to bring harmony to this planet. Be kind to the animals that you are the keeper of, for these creatures are also a part of the Source, and they too, have souls such as you have souls. Be kind and loving to the creatures that God has placed in your care, and know that your pets are in your life to teach you a lesson of love as well.

There exists on the planet, what you would term as the food chain. Be aware that this food chain maintains the balance of the planet. Every insect has a prey, and it keeps their balance and maintains their sustenance. If unchecked, your planet would fall out of balance. Mammals too, have preys, and they maintain their balance as such. Be aware of this.

I'm not sure I understand the point you are trying to make here.

Melanie: When we speak of balance, we speak of the mutual agreement between all species for mutual survival. When mankind upsets this balance, he is doing a great disservice to the planet and all of life it contains. An animal hunts when it is hungry, and it does not waste its food source. Mankind hunts merely, at times, for his frivolous desires. Early man wore fur skins for protection against the elements, but modern man wears furs for mere frivolity. It is not acceptable to upset the balance in this way. It is not acceptable to hunt animals for merely one part of their body and toss away the carcass. Your animals are becoming extinct, and your forests are dying due to mankind's self serving, frivolous nature. This is not done out of love for each other and for the love of the planet, but it is done out of mankind's frivolous and misguided love of ego; not to be confused with love of spiritual self.

When you prey on an animal for sustenance, you sustain your vessel or body, as you would term it. When you hunt for hunting's sake, you disrespect that which would sustain you. If you are a meat eater, respect the animals that would sustain you, and treat them kindly and remember that they have an awareness too. Love these animals and respect them.

When speaking of animal extinction and upsetting the natural balance, there are those who would argue, in the case of animal furs for example, that some animals are raised specifically for this purpose, as is done with minks.

Minks are a loving animal who feel love towards their offspring and hurt when their loved ones are taken away and massacred. You are the keeper of this planet in a sense because you have conscious intelligent self-awareness. Be kind and loving towards all animals and people. You have many times shown love towards animals in distress and healed or saved their lives. Make sure to show love towards all creatures and this planet as well. And remember that in this love, you will respect the entire planet and promote its longevity and well being.

You tell us that we are the keepers of animals and to be loving towards them, yet some of them are a part of our food chain. How can we reconcile this?

Meat is a staple of the human body, for it provides protein which is a building block of humans and animals. Meat is necessary for protein, and when we spoke of the cooperation between the species of the food chain, your meat is a part of this cooperation. Many tribes of people and your ancestors as well, understand this connection, and they respect what is God given to them. Many of them give prayers of thanks and perform rituals of thanks for this food. It is important that when life is taken of the food chain, it is done so with respect towards the animal that is sustaining you. Make an effort to take life humanely and not carelessly. This animal is a gift, and gifts are not to be taken lightly or for granted. The tradition of praying before a meal, to give thanks to the Source and to the animal who gave his life for you, is an example of the traditional ritual of what we speak.

Many times, you take life frivolously away. You hunt for trophies and glamour, and you are hunting and fishing to the extinction of your food supplies. Love and respect what God has given you. This is what we mean by being a care taker of animals. Some animals are your loving pets and companions. Love them and they will, in turn, teach you the value of unconditional love. Other animals are part of your food chain. Love and respect what they are giving you. Take life only when you need it, and waste not and plunder not, needlessly, for you will affect the loving balance of this wonderful planet that the Source has provided for you.

I don't mean to turn this into a chapter on healthy eating, but when you speak of animals being a necessary protein, this is somewhat contradictory to a comment you made previously, where you stated that we should eliminate red meat.

Red meat is fatty and heavy on your digestive system. It is to be used sparingly if you do not eliminate it. There are leaner sources that are better for you.

Love, you see, connects us all, and without love we would cease to exist. Love is the Source, and the Source is love which is pure light and energy. If we think, hypothetically, about it, we could ascertain that if love expired, then the Source would cease to exist, and with that, we would simply cease to exist.

Love is pure, unconditional, and everlasting. It cannot be eliminated. It can turn hate and apathy around by washing over it and transforming it. Make no mistake when we tell you that love is the basis for all existence. If you could experience the depth of love that emanates from the Source, your lives on Earth would be changed in an instant.

Meditate, and many fruits will come to you.

Chapter Eight:

Laughter

Em: We would like to impress upon you that laughter has many qualities that you all take for granted. It is an expression of joy and love that emanates from within the soul of each person on this planet. It expresses joy, and it expresses one's feelings of love contained within joy. Laughter is an expression that lightens a heavy soul and helps to ease sorrow in times of pain. Many would benefit from the expression of laughter; laughter at a joke, laughter at laying eyes on a loved one, or laughter as the expression of a joyous soul. Make an attempt to include laughter in your lives, for the uplifting qualities of laughter add joy to your heart. It can be utilized to break silences that are heavy with sadness in order to lift up the essence of humanity. It can affect the healing of a sad heart or introduce lightheartedness into an otherwise dull situation. The process of laughter, itself, can lighten up the feelings within you. It is the expression of a joyous soul, and it is the gift the Source has given you to express the joy contained within you.

    Melanie: Laughter is the road to a content and happy soul. When you engage in lightheartedness, you bring good health and happiness to yourself and others. When you laugh, you raise your vibrations, which, in turn, heal and sustain your body's good health. Laughter raises your good energy and the energy of others.

You say that laughter raises our vibrations. Can you explain how this works?

We vibrate at a specific vibrational level, and laughter helps to raise our vibrational frequencies. Laughter raises these frequencies by instilling a positive lightheartedness within us. Humans vibrate at a lower level than spiritual beings, which causes your density. When the human spirit engages in laughter, these vibrations are raised, and as a result, they are felt throughout the body, and these raised frequencies are helpful in the good health of an individual.

So, what I understand from this is that positive emotions vibrate at higher frequencies which, in turn, cause us to vibrate at higher frequencies, and the higher the frequencies we vibrate at, the healthier we are.

Yes, this is exactly it. Make sure to include laughter in your daily life.

Out of curiosity, what is the general range of frequencies that humans vibrate at, and what is the general range of frequencies that a spiritual entity, such as your self, vibrates at?

Many humans vibrate at what you would term to be the mid range. This range is low enough to support mass without breaking it apart, yet high enough so that mankind can still occupy mass without evaporating the molecules into spirit. Your spirit must lower its vibration to match the vibration of your body's mass, allowing the spirit and body to lock into position. Lower ranges can actually cause harm to the human body. Very low vibrational frequencies, such as very low and deep rumbling type frequencies, can disrupt the matter and mass of the human body. There are frequencies that are so deep and low that they can disrupt solid mass and cause it to break apart. These vibrations are such that mass is disrupted as a result of their vibrational pattern.

If you could visualize a vibration, it would appear as a wave. A very high frequency would appear as a solid line due to the extremely fast movement of the wave. A very deep and low frequency would appear as a very large tidal wave, and this wave would be large and powerful, and hard hitting. If you think of mass as atoms and molecules, you will see that mass is not as solid as it appears; therefore, a very deep and low frequency could quite easily disrupt the molecules and cause them to scatter. We, who are your guides, vibrate at what you would term to be a very high frequency.

Is it within our hearing range?

No, we must lower our frequencies to be seen and heard by you. When we lower our frequencies, it is for the purpose of inhabiting your dimension. We do this, at times, to make ourselves visible to you in solid form. It does not trap us here or affect us adversely, for we are not of your dimension. There are times when man is in need and mysterious strangers appear to assist and then they leave without notice. This would be an example of our manifestation.

Does laughter affect you the same way it affects us?

Yes, laughter is good for all souls.

How does laughter affect our health in a positive manner?

Have you noticed that it is impossible to laugh and feel sad at the same time? Make a test for your self to prove this point, and the next time you are engaged in laughter, check and see the feelings associated with it. You will notice a good feeling washing over yourself; and make this a daily habit. When you engage others in laughter, it does the same for them, and it will help to raise their vibration as well. Be sure to invite it into your life, and you will be able to best deal with life's stresses also because laughter helps to release stress, and that will help to promote good health.

When you are feeling sad, find something to make you laugh, and your mood will be uplifted. You have the ability to think yourself happy; and it is a gift from the Source, for every parent loves to see their children's happiness, and laughter is truly infectious. Have you noticed at times, that someone's laughter has infectiously caused others around him to break into laughter even though they know not the reason why? This laughter puts everyone into an immediate state of well being.

The laughter you engage in affects your body on a molecular level and causes changes inside your body and mind as well as your soul. Laughter will alter your molecular composition, and this is how it affects your health in a positive manner. Be aware of this, and allow your heart to invite laughter into your heart and the heart of others.

Molecules are energy, just as you are. The matter that is you is comprised of millions upon millions of molecules. Laughter promotes good health by bathing these molecules in positive, healing energy. Just as negative energy promotes illness, positive energy promotes good health. Laughter generates positive energy that has a positive revitalizing effect on your molecules. Laughter raises the vibrational quality of these molecules and bathes them in what you refer to as good energy. This is none other than the magnetism that powers all, and it is the energy supplied by the Source, which is healing in its essence to molecules that are being affected by negative energy produced by a discordant mind.

Em: You have the ability to make your reality shift through a major or minor shift in your mood. If you shift your mood mildly, you can begin to shift your well being in your life. You can also shift your mood greatly, and many shifts will occur within yourself. It is as simple as putting a smile on your face or breaking into great laughter. Your mood can be affected by something as simple as a smile.

You state that we have the ability to make our reality shift through a major or minor shift in our mood. How can minor or major shifts in our moods cause shifts in our realities?

Moods are energy also, and they can be negative or positive. Moods can shift your reality by contributing either positive or negative energy, depending on your emotions. Laughter offers a positive shift through the law of magnetism, which you term the law of attraction. It is very simple. Like attracts like, good attracts good, and bad attracts bad. This is how your moods can shift your realities.

How can something as simple as a smile affect our mood?

Make an attempt to smile, and automatically it produces an effect in your solar plexus that is pleasant. Try to smile and be angry. It is almost impossible. Make yourself smile next time you are feeling sad, by thinking about something pleasant. If you do this simple exercise to uplift your mood, it will continue to cause a shift inside your soul. If you cannot make yourself laugh, then this smiling exercise is the first step. Continue to do this exercise whenever your mood is blue. Eventually, you can graduate to making yourself laugh, and this will eventually allow you to break into laughter when you are down. You will find that laughter will eventually come easier to you on a regular basis. Eventually, you will acquire a naturally happy disposition in life. You will create a healthy shift inside your mind and body. Find the time to do this every day.

Can a simple smile or laughter help us if we are sad, or angry, or if our hearts have been broken? Can a smile or laughter work if we are feeling this way?

Yes, it can. Learn to smile when your heart is broken, and this will help to shift your mood because a smile causes physiological changes in your body structure. Remember that song, "smile though your heart is aching?" It has truth.

Sometimes when you are in that much pain, it is really difficult to force a smile, and you feel like you just want to experience the sorrow you are feeling.

Make yourself think happy thoughts. If you are dealing with a death or a breakup, make yourself think of happy memories of your loved one, and this will help your healing. Meditation can help you achieve a level of tranquility and calm disposition. This can help to center you so that you can create this level of lightheartedness in an easier manner. When you achieve this level of lightheartedness, laughter comes more easily to you. Meditation is the most important practice you can adopt for the most malleable manner to adjust your lightheartedness. It is through thought and meditation that you can allow a change in your belief system. It is your belief system that can be your greatest enemy. Meditation helps you to mold yourself.

We spoke about the molecular shift that laughter can create within your cellular level. This is a very real and tangible shift. The good vibrations that laughter creates, washes over your entire cellular and molecular level and causes minute changes at this level that are contagious to the surrounding molecules and cells. This chain reaction has a domino effect on your cellular structure and it can literally cure your ailment as these cells transform and repair themselves while eliminating diseases within the structure of these cells.

You talk about how laughter can cure ailments and heal diseases within the structures of our cells. Can you explain how these changes occur on a cellular, structural level?

Yes. Energy, as we said. It is energy that empowers everything. The energy provided by the Source. It empowers us all. Energy can be utilized to heal, for just as words that are spoken lovingly can make us feel good, so can loving energy wash over us and affect our cellular level, for within this cellular level, lies the energy that powers us all. Make it a habit to include laughter in your lives, for laughter brings happiness, and happiness is a positive vibrational state that affects our cells through its good vibrations and this can cause healing, just as negative energy can cause illness.

Meditate for your good health, and bring joy and laughter into your heart and soul, and the rest will follow.

Make a list of things that make you laugh, and use this list to trigger you when you want to laugh. As you become more practiced, you will be able to break into laughter more easily. Be aware that you have memories that you can draw from, and use this well of memories also. You may also create new laughter in your life by attending to your many light hearted functions, such as comedic movies and comedy clubs.

Melanie: Laughter is infectious, and in a group such as one at a comedy venue, you will notice that the merriment in the room creates a vibrational change in all who are in attendance. A person who is just entering that room would notice a lighter and charged room of people.

You are making light hearted memories every day. Make it a habit to have fun and laughter in your life, and you will continue to affect your mental and physical health in a positive way. Do this and you will notice the results. You should attempt to bring laughter into the lives of others also, for what you send to others will also return to you.

Make sure you attend to laughter on a regular basis, and you will be promoting your good health.

Laughter

Chapter Nine:

Emotions

Melanie: Your emotions are the barometer of your soul. They tell you if you are happy or sad, depressed or elated, and they indicate whether your decisions are right or wrong. Make no mistake; your emotions are very important to your well being, and your guide to many of life's directions. You have been born with all the emotions necessary to guide you through your life.

Emotions are the expressions of your soul as expressed through the human organic body, and they are based on pure guttural expression as translated through your dimensional existence. The filters of your human condition however, translate some emotions purely based on negative expression, which we refer to as emotions of the low order. Although many would expect love to be the only expression of the soul due to its direct connection to the Source, you must remember that the low frequency of your dimension as well as the current evolutionary state of mankind allows for a range of soul expressions on your level, ranging from love to hatred.

As a baby, your emotions were your way to communicate your needs to your parents. When you were hungry, you cried because this hunger made you emotional. When you were frustrated, you became emotional. When you needed your diaper changed, your emotions communicated this to your parents; so you see, you have been very attached to your soul from birth, and as you became an adult, you were trained to keep your emotions at bay and repressed.

Emotions are the language of the soul and through them, mankind gains entry to his soul. The ego is not a part of your emotional soul, although it utilizes fear to its advantage. The soul speaks through emotion, and through emotion, you are connected to your soul.

As children, you continued to express yourself through emotions, and this was now coupled with your vocabulary, and you were able to express yourself in a clearer manner. Your childhood expressions were directly linked to your emotions, and you made every effort to relay your opinions in an emotional way, although, not as a baby.

Children are more connected to their emotions and better able to express them because they do not feel self conscious about doing so. Many children have a healthier disposition than adults as a result of this. Your emotions, when heeded and acted upon, will help to level your many moods that would cause you illness due to their repression. Your emotions are the soul's method of communicating with you, and when you heed these communications, you will assist your development in life. Make meditation your guide to reconnect with your emotions again.

How does repressing our emotions cause illness?

Making yourself repress emotions is to deny yourself and your soul the right to be a sentient being. Making yourself numb is not productive to your spirit's progress, and by stuffing our emotions by not validating what we feel, we can cause harm to our bodies. An example of this is the obese person who stuffs his body with food because he is stuffing his emotions and refusing to face the root of what is causing him to feel pain. We are not suggesting that this is the case with all obese people. When you acknowledge your feelings, you are allowing your soul the freedom of its expression. We are not suggesting that you act upon all of your emotions, but rather, acknowledge them and discover their cause.

When your emotions are repressed, they fester like an unresolved wound or boil. Emotions carry energy, and depending on the type of emotion felt, this energy is either positive or negative. Repressing emotions and not embracing their existence or cause, can allow them to seek resolution within the organic body. The energy has no where or no means to express itself and turns itself inwards upon the body. This can lead to illness and disease. By acknowledging your emotions and either giving them expression or thought, you are allowing the release of energy, and this release can be therapeutic if the emotions are negative and require your attention. Repressed energy must go somewhere, for energy seeks transformation, and illness is the result of the transformation of unresolved and repressed energy.

Make a list of the emotions you experience, and determine what events in your life they are connected to. This will help to resolve problems and issues in your life by making you aware of their existence.

Your emotions are a very important part of your life, and without them, you would make many wrong decisions and judgment calls necessary to your well being. You have only to look at people who are disconnected from themselves, and you will notice that they always seem to make bad decisions that lead them into unfortunate circumstances. Be aware of your feelings and the thoughts connected to them. Be also aware of what these thoughts and emotions are communicating to you. You have many emotions that help to direct the course of your life.

Is there a difference between our feelings and our emotions? I feel that we should be guided by our feelings rather than our emotions.

Make no mistake that there is a distinction, but your emotions are indicators of what you are feeling and thinking, so therefore, they should be acknowledged.

Is it our thoughts that cause our emotions?

Many thoughts can cause many emotions. Sad thoughts cause sadness, angry thoughts cause anger, and so forth. You are connected in body, and soul, and thought.

If that's the case then shouldn't we use our emotions as a way of analyzing our thoughts and beliefs. If it's our thoughts and beliefs that are causing our emotions, and we're experiencing negative emotions, then maybe this means that we should be analyzing our thoughts and beliefs.

Yes. Meditation is a good way to connect with the Source as well as with your self, and your thoughts are exactly what your beliefs are based upon. Your thoughts and beliefs are the foundation that your life is built upon. As mentioned in the chapter on beliefs, some of these beliefs are so deeply engrained that you are not even aware, consciously, of their deep imprint upon your life. It is through examining your emotions that many of you can begin to peel away the layers of your mind where these beliefs are buried. Your emotions serve as a good indicator of what lies within your subconscious mind. Utilize these emotions as a tool to rediscover your engrained beliefs and to analyze the thoughts that accompany these beliefs. You will discover a portion of yourself that has been buried for years.

(To Tina and Tilde: Your next sessions will delve into the various emotions that you have. Make sure that you are rested.)

Love

Em: You are all children of God. God being the Source, and as children of the Source, you are here on Earth to experience lessons in the physical realm, and the emotions and feelings that you experience have a direct impact on these lessons, and they are indicators of how you are progressing in the school of life on this plane. Make an effort to be aware of these emotions and their relevance in your life. Make sure that the emotions that guide you are true to your essence and soul, and that you entertain the emotions of the highest order, which is love, and that you analyze the emotions of the lower order, and determine what they are trying to teach you.

How do we know if the emotions that guide us are true to our essence and soul?

We know if they are true due to their resonance within us. If it feels right then it must be so, but if it is not right, your soul will feel a sense of being off center. Many times, you have gone against your better judgment or, shall we say, intuition, only to discover that you should have heeded this feeling in the first place. You will know by how it resonates within you. Your emotions are your barometer. If you feel sad, there has to be a reason why. If you are angry, there has to be a reason why. Allow yourself to be connected to your emotions as a baby is connected, but not in the literal sense, for you have developed beyond your babyhood.

You say that our emotions are our guidance system, but shouldn't we use logic to guide us rather than our emotions? Doesn't emotional thinking stop you from making rational decisions? Once again this leads me back to the sense that we should be guided by our feelings rather than our emotions.

We understand what you are saying, but think of the many times you ignored your instincts and allowed your logic to screw things up.

To my way of thinking, I feel that emotions are almost tainted in a way because of their lack of logic.

We are not referring to childish emotional behaviors, but rather, think of it as emotional logic.

You'll need to explain that to me because those are two opposite ends of the spectrum by my thinking.

Yes, we know, but what we are trying to tell you is more simple than you realize. An animal has not your logic, yet an animal functions better than you at times because it relies on instinct. Your instinct has many flavors. These flavors are the flavors of emotion. Fear is an emotion, yet it can be helpful in times of distress. It can kick you into action that is required.

Okay, I see what you're saying . That's beginning to make more sense to me. Now, previously you mentioned that emotions are indicators of how we are navigating our lives. How is this so?

They are indicators because they alert you to how you are navigating. If you are sad, then ask yourself "what did you do to cause or allow the sadness?" Yes, it is all a matter of cause and effect. What caused the effect? What did you do to cause the effect? How did your navigation of your life, get you to a point that caused sadness?

Perhaps it's something as simple as my beliefs or my thoughts. Don't we have a choice? I could choose to be sad in any given situation, or I could choose to not be sad.

Yes. Make no mistake; it all comes back to you. Make sure to allow yourself to let your emotions speak to you, for if you analyze them, you can get to the bottom of whatever is affecting you.

Couldn't you just choose to not be sad, and then problem solved?

No. It is not that simple, for humans are complicated. If your arm was cut off, could you simply refuse to acknowledge it?

Very good point, but I guess I'm thinking of a more simple example than that. Suppose someone is in a bad mood. They could just choose to not be in a bad mood.

No, and yes. You could choose to not be in a bad mood, but if you don't allow yourself to discover why you are in a bad mood, then you are simply applying a band-aid to an open wound. Find out what is wounding you, and heal it first. Laughter is something we have recommended that will help, but it is more than a band-aid that you must apply.

Melanie: You are an emotional being, and these emotions are your guidance system in life. Emotions range from the highest order to the lowest order, and they are indicators of how you are navigating your life, and they also serve as beacons or indicators of your emotional state. Make sure that you are connected to your emotions, and be aware of the messages they are sending you. Make sure to meditate and become connected to your emotional self, for this is your way of connecting to the Source state.

Earlier, you mentioned that we are emotional beings, but then you also stated that we are sentient beings. Can you explain what you mean? What is the difference?

By sentient, we mean that you have a conscious awareness as well as an understanding awareness of your world as it pertains to your beliefs and dimension, whereas emotions are more related to your sense of feeling. Emotions are different in that they are the barometers of your soul, but as sentient beings, you have an awareness that is deeper than emotional. You have an awareness that is spiritual because of your connection to the Source. Make it a habit to meditate, and through meditation, you will become in tune with your sentient self.

You are a sentient being, and the Source expresses itself through you on this plane. You are God's voice on Earth; therefore, you must strive for achievement of the highest order. Love is the highest order, and it is the highest emotional state that you can achieve. Love, in its purest form, is all encompassing and purely unconditional. Be aware of this goal, and make love the driving force and ambition behind all your goals and endeavors.

Unconditional love seems like such an unattainable goal. How can we possibly strive towards this ideal?

In your reality, it does seem unattainable, and it is because of this that there is a journey of repeated reincarnations. We would advise you to continue to meditate. We know that we have continued to repeat meditation, but it is for a valid purpose. In meditation, you will eventually attain a purity of connection that will open your third eye, and once this eye is open, you will have access to the pure love energy of the Source. This energy will impart the loving ideal emotion that we all strive to attain. We would also advise you to be aware of the human bond of connection that you all share, and in this bond, realize that you also share common love, fear, sorrow, compassion, and so forth. When you look at another human being, try to see yourself and your loved ones in that person, for you truly share many common traits. We all are the same in the Source's mind.

We spoke of love in a previous chapter, and we begin this list of emotions with love as the first and foremost emotion. You are here for love and love alone. Every other lesson and emotion is meant to steer you towards love lessons. Your emotions are the indicators that let you know whether or not you are on your true course. Love is the God Source in all its glory, and love is the emotion that your soul is striving to reconnect with again in this physical plane.

You make every effort, at times, to run away from love. You make every effort, at times, to exclude love from your lives. You make every effort, at times, to downplay its importance, but always know that the lessons on this Earth are meant to connect you to love.

Why is it so difficult for us to reconnect with love again, on this physical plane?

It is difficult for many of you because of the nature of your reality. You vibrate at a lower level than us, and as a result, the density that you inhabit affects you in such a manner because you are not directly spiritually connected to the Source as the souls that inhabit our plane. This density makes it more challenging as a result of this perceived disconnection. It is not only dense in human body, but it is also dense in human thought and emotion, for this density affects both. Many of you are able to achieve a level of purity also because making the transition to purity of self and soul is your quest in this lifetime. Many of you who are able to achieve this purity have done so because you are on your final leg of reincarnation and are ready to graduate to a higher or next level.

Love is not as elusive as you say it is. Love should be the easiest emotion to attain, but you complicate it by putting conditions on it. Conditional love is what you end up with, and this is why love is elusive to many of you. Conditional love can never attain unconditional status can it? You must try to remember that love in its purest form has no conditions or strings attached to it. Make it a daily practice to find something in everyone that you can love about them. By seeing loving qualities in people, you can open your heart to give love and to receive it in kind. Love will truly set you free, as the saying goes.

Love has healing qualities, for when you emanate love, you give out emotional energy of the highest order, and this pure emotion carries with it the healing qualities of the white light of the Source, whose connection you are emanating. You see that the connection with this Source, in a loving manner, helps you to achieve enlightenment and to maintain the health of the planet you dwell on. You have accomplished many great healings in the light of the love emotional energy, and this is evident in many countries in which you have lovingly helped in your missionary quests.

Make room for meditation on the love emotion, for this is the path to true enlightenment. Mother Teresa is a great example of love, healing, and enlightenment, but a good example also, of love without conditions. She continues to express this love and healing towards your planet even though she has undergone a physical death, as you would term it. Make no mistake about the fact that your growth continues even after death, as you term it, but we will go into that in another chapter.

Your love lessons on this plane are meant to make you aware of your fellow humans in a manner that makes all who give and receive love aware of a higher purpose for us all.

Em: Make room in your mind for loving thoughts towards others, for these thoughts will take root in your lives and create an energy of good will towards others. These loving thoughts will encompass the planet, for loving thoughts create loving gestures and acts towards others which will in turn cause others to react in kind. By bathing others in loving energy, you can cause their internal energies to shift in a positive direction. Have you ever been cruel to someone when you feel love towards them? Have you been cruel to someone when you feel negative towards them? By feeling and expressing love towards others, you can create internal shifts of positive energy that will create this domino effect towards others. The act of being loving towards others is infectious and love can conquer in ways that wars and hatred never will.

Loving thoughts should not be limited towards people, but should be expanded to include the whole planet. Animals have souls and emotions as well, and should be included in your sphere of love. Animals can sense love, and they can sense your will towards them, whether it be loving or not. Animals that you keep as pets are examples of unconditional love for you. They love you and show it without reservations. Many hospitals and homes are beginning to recognize the healing that love brings in the patients that this therapy is applied to.

Love energy towards the planet will bring healing to the planet itself, for this love will cause humanity to be a better caretaker of the planet and all its creatures and life forms. Love can cause a loving change. Remember that as souls, in the beginning of your time, you created this planet to experience life for your greater good and learning. Learn through love, and grow with love. Make this a daily habit, and your life will transform itself in ways you never imagined. Your planet is to go through a major shift and love will get you through it.

Our planet is about to go through a major shift? What is this shift, and how will love help to get us through it?

We are saving the bulk of this material for another book, but will elaborate a little.

Your planet has had many shifts in its long history, and many more are in its future. These are all a part of your Earth evolution; some of which are natural and some of which are induced by mankind's existence and tampering with the Earth's natural state of being. Your Earth has shifted poles in the past, and will shift poles again in the future.

Mankind has tampered with the Earth in ways that Earth has not experienced before. The detonation of bombs has disrupted Earth's natural energy shield, and the mining of vast geographical areas has caused shifts in the Earth's crust that have resulted in some of your natural disasters. It is only logical that there would be consequences and reactions to mankind's tampering of the planet. We would urge you to seek peaceful means of coexistence and natural means of energy that would replace your destructive tilling and mining of your planet.

We would advise you to come together as a loving humanity to ensure the continuation of your species upon this planet. By coming together in love, you will survive, but if you become a fearful, covetous race during this period, you will do much harm unto your species. Think of how tragedies have brought people together in the past and how this togetherness has rebuilt all of that which was demolished. This is the way, and love will get you through it.

Melanie: Love, you see, is the unifying force in the Universe, and it binds us together through connection with the Source. Whether you agree or disagree, you cannot be without love, for to be without love causes much discontent and disagreement within oneself. You are here through love, and love is your ultimate goal. Be aware of love in your life, and seek to find ways in which you can include it in the lives of others as well. We urge you to meditate on love and on spiritual cleansing.

Love is the ultimate emotion of the highest order, and this is the key to true enlightenment.

Compassion

The next emotion we want to talk about is compassion. Always be compassionate towards one another, for it is through compassion that love can take root and blossom. Be aware of each other, and be aware of each other's feelings. It is said that to understand another it is important to walk in his shoes. This is the path to compassion. Make sure that you practice this on a daily basis and you will understand each other more fully. Being compassionate towards one another is an emotion of a high order that leads to emotions of the highest order through compassionate connections with each other. To be truly compassionate is to understand each other's feelings in the fullest way and to sympathize with each other in times of need and sorrow.

Make it a natural effort to practice compassion and to make it a natural part of your personality. Be compassionate to the planet and all of its inhabitants. Compassion can build bridges of understanding and avert anger and wars with one another. You are a race that holds firmly to its belief systems and because of this, there is much strife on your planet.

Make a list of the different cultures that exist on your planet, and you will have a list of the many belief systems and ideologies that exist in your world. You are all fighting so hard to maintain that your way is the right way, that you don't stop to acknowledge that you could all be right within your own beliefs. You are now immediately wondering about the ideologies of those who would kill and terrorize for their beliefs. Know that you could hold your beliefs without the necessity of harming one another for them. To kill another is to harm yourself as well, for to kill another is to kill your connection to the Source.

When we speak of killing your connection to the Source, we speak of it in terms of estrangement. Your Source soul connection cannot be killed in the literal sense, but there are many among you who have estranged yourselves and lost your true sense of divinity. Make love, not war, as your saying goes. By this, we mean that you should always go forth with love in your hearts. True compassion is an avenue to love.

Compassion allows you to have a common bond with your fellow human being, and in this compassion, you can also see yourself. When you can make that connection and realize that you are all brothers and sisters, then you can begin to rebuild the bridges of love that once existed between all of humanity. Make sure that you use compassion when you are dealing with each other in your lives, for this will truly bring love and peace to your world.

Make time for compassion for one another, for compassion leads to understanding, and understanding leads to love. When you have compassion, it will give you an understanding for one another's beliefs and ideologies, thus leading to an awareness of the reasons for all your differences on Earth, and it will cause you to feel compassion and the desire to become a part of the solution in a loving way. The path to enlightenment is filled with many lessons and tests, and throughout your journey you will come across many others whose purpose is to help your growth, just as your purpose in their lives is the same. Your compassion for one another will help this growth for all concerned. Make many friends, for friends will lead to understanding our differences, and we will learn that our differences will aid in our growth when we add compassion to the mix.

Love and compassion are integrated emotions, for to have love for one another is to have compassion as well, and to have compassion is to be able to access feelings of love in connection to compassion. Your capacity for compassion is great, and you have only to open your heart for each other in order to connect with your compassion for each other.

Make it a habit to open your minds of connection for your fellow human beings, and you will begin to notice that your levels of compassion will grow for each other. You have the capacity, as a human race, to attain such greatness and levels of achievement, but you thwart it through hatred and inconsideration for each other and the planet as a whole. You see, hatred and inconsideration are the flip side emotions of love and compassion, but we will touch on these in good time. Through love and compassion, all the other emotions of the highest order spring forth. You see that because of love and compassion in your lives, you are able to experience joy, happiness, forgiveness, empathy, and many other emotions of the high and highest order. Practice these emotions on a daily basis for your spiritual growth.

Em: Compassion for one another would help to alleviate the hatred and anxiety towards each other. By feeling compassion for another, it is easier to facilitate a greater understanding for each other's feelings and points of view. By feeling what another feels and understanding another's point of view, you could more easily come to agreements with each other through compassion and understanding without the need for oppression and war to solve your differences. Try to practice this in your daily life when situations of disagreements occur. Compassion will allow you to change places with each other and will, in turn, give you a sympathetic and compassionate view point with each other. You can alleviate suffering through compassion as well. When you see people who are less fortunate than yourself, you should try to be compassionate rather than judgmental towards your fellow souls. You are better off helping through compassion rather than judging through fear and ignorance.

Mother Teresa is a true example of this. She saw the essence of God in even the lowliest persons of your societies. Through her love and compassion, she dedicated herself to applying love, and tended with compassion to all souls she helped. She realized that her holiness was no different than that of the leper or beggar. These souls assist us in discovering the lessons of love and compassion in our lives. These people are not invisible. These people are your brothers and sisters, and the lessons they impart are invaluable.

Your spirituality is affected through your ability to be compassionate with one another. Allow yourself the mental dedication to practice compassion towards those who you would classify as the lower classes of your society. Their purpose in your life is a noble one, for it is their presence in your life that allows you to grow spiritually through the application of compassion.

Your spiritual growth is desirable on this plane of existence. Everyone has a purpose and a path to follow. Allow yourself to be open to accepting and giving compassion, for this will allow growth for all concerned.

Be with God and live in love essence, for this is where we all come from and will all eventually strive to return to. We love you all and feel the utmost compassion for you all.

Joy

Melanie: Joy is the next emotion we will discuss. Joy is an emotion of the highest order and can best be described as an intense level of pure happiness. When we experience unconditional love, we open our souls to the joy that it brings, for to be in a state of love that is pure, is to be in a state of joy. Love is joy, and joy is felt through the experience of allowing ourselves to express this emotion. Many of you may be wondering what we mean, and many of you might be confused by this.

Joy is the expression of love realized by the soul, just as sorrow would be the expression and feeling of hatred and despair. To be joyous is to realize the true meaning and depth of love. It has no higher expression. The joyous soul expresses love and the loving soul expresses joy. These two go hand in hand. How many times have you seen people truly in love, express their exuberant joy? We urge mankind to discover his joy and his love.

You are meant to experience life's lessons in order to attain spiritual awareness, and in that discovery, you will find your way to the Source, which is love. The joy that is felt is the expression of the soul in its discovery and connection to love. The pain of childbirth is quickly forgotten and replaced by the feeling of joy when a mother instantly falls in love with her new baby. A mother's joy is the true happy expression of her soul at the love connection she feels towards her baby. Love is the path to joy, and joy is a path of love and to love, for to have love in your heart is to experience the joy that love can bring.

Make a mental note of all the times you have felt joy in your life, and determine what this joy was related to. You will discover that feelings of love have been connected to this joy, and that the joy itself causes feelings of love.

How can we bring joy into our lives? Day to day living can be so hard and challenging for many of us. What do we need to do to open ourselves to attracting it into our lives?

This is true of your reality. We would again advise meditation as a start. Let meditation guide you to the lake of joy that exists within the Source. Let this joy wash over you. On a daily basis, we would advise you to realize all that you have to be thankful for. You have the beauty of a sunrise. You have the beauty of a star lit night. You have a roof over your head. You have so much to be thankful for, and yet you take these things for granted. If you have not sight, be thankful for your hearing. If you have not your hearing, be thankful for the loving people who help you to hear with sign language. Much has been developed in your world that many should be thankful for. When you can begin to see the beauty in the smallest thing that exists, you will be able to open your heart in joy and thanks for all that the Source has provided you with.

Many go through life without noticing or realizing the true miracle of creation. Even the smallest particle that exists is a miracle of creation. Stop and smell the roses, has deeper meaning than mankind realizes. Take time in your day to contemplate the miracles of creation that surround you. Breathe the air and be thankful and joyful for the life it gives you. Smell the flowers and be joyful for the beautiful essences they impart. Mankind has much to be joyful and thankful for. When mankind focuses on the beauty of life, he will have a harder time extinguishing it.

Joy is the natural state of the soul. When your soul leaves its body and returns to the Source, it returns to a state of pure unconditional love and joy. When we discover this joy on Earth, we are returning to our natural God and divine level that is rightfully our natural soul state. You don't need to experience an Earthly death to be in this state of grace.

You are here in this plane to experience and achieve a natural soul state through the knowledge that you attain here. Your journey on this level serves to make the soul aware of itself and to make it achieve a state of knowledge, love, and joy through its experiences. When you are on the right path in life, your emotions serve as your guidance system, and joy is the result when your path of life is true and loving towards yourself and fellow Source souls.

You state that love and joy will be the result of our decisions if our path is true, but isn't it possible that a decision that brings us joy isn't necessarily a good decision for us? As an example, quitting my job might bring me joy, but I'd suddenly be left without an income.

When one door closes another one opens, and the door that opens may be the one that is meant to bring you joy.

Demna: Your path, in a sense, has been predetermined, but only as far as the conditions that you were brought into. By this, we mean conditions such as the parents you chose and the life style that you were born into. In all else, you have free will, and this means that the outcome of your experience is determined by the free will that you exercise. We will delve into this further, but in relationship to emotions, your free will determines which experiences you choose to experience. If these experiences do not bring you love and joy, then it is important to examine where your free will is leading you and determine the changes you must make. Love and joy should be the guiding emotions for your soul because through love, the soul is guided towards its ultimate goal, and joy is the expression of pure happiness that the soul feels when its path is true and its core is love. When you are on your path, let your emotions be your barometer in pursuing this path. Your emotions will let you know if your decisions feel right and if the circumstances you find yourself in are right, with love and joy being the result of your decisions if your path is true. You will never steer yourself into the wrong direction if you listen to the inner voice of knowledge and reason that is the voice of God within you. You all have God's voice within you, and it is the voice of intuitive reasoning. Listen to this voice, and follow its guidance towards a fuller life of love, joy, compassion, and understanding towards you and your fellow Source souls. Love be with you all.

Melanie: Love and joy are emotions of the highest order and the emotional goal of the soul. Other emotions will help to guide us through life's journey, and obstacles, and lessons. They may not be of the highest order, but many are considered to be a necessary part of the inner communication of the Source voice.

Our next emotion is.......

Fear

You have all had feelings of fear, and sometimes this fear is unfounded, and sometimes it serves to prevent you from entering situations that might endanger you. It is important to discern within yourself, whether the fear is founded or not. Listen to your inner voice, for it will help to guide you. Your fear, if used properly, will benefit you in times of potential danger, but will hold you back if it is unreasonable. Listen to your inner voice, and meditate every day so you can focus on your inner dialogue with the God Source. Make it a daily dialogue, and make it a natural one, for the Source is always with you and within you.

Fear is unfounded when it is irrational, and will lead you away from the lessons and discoveries in your life. Is the fear you experience towards a given situation based on making you stand still in your journey, or is it guiding you away from a harmful situation? If it is making you fearful because you feel unsure of a direction or goal that you desire, then ask yourself, "what is the true reason for this fear?" Make the fear go away if it is holding you back from progress that is pure for you. This is easier said than done, as you would term it, and for many of you, this is true. Many times, the fear is due to personal doubts and insecurity, and is tied to your belief systems that are holding you back. If this is the case, then re-read the chapter on belief, and you can begin to analyze why this is so in your life. You can change your beliefs around your fear, and in that process, you can re-establish your connection to your true path in life. If you can alter your fear through altering the beliefs connected to it, you can put your life into a forward gear, and it will make a difference in your life. Most of the fear we have is attached to our belief systems, and by altering these beliefs, we will dissipate the fear and move through it and forward into the life we are meant to have. Make it a habit to work through your irrational fears, for they will bind you and hold you back.

Irrational fear is a fear based on imagined or false assumptions about a given situation. This fear is destructive and unproductive in a person's life. If you can determine the beliefs surrounding a given fear, you can then analyze its root and you can begin to work at addressing it and eliminating it from your life. It is in your mind, and you must change the way you perceive the reality and beliefs surrounding the fear in order to eliminate it from your life.

The mind is a powerful tool, and the ego, at times, operates out of fear; not of what is, but of what may be. The purpose of the ego is survival of self, and this ego is prone to irrational fears. Fears are also a product of mental conditioning throughout one's lifetime. Our parents, and many who we meet in life, contribute to our beliefs. As children, your beliefs are dependent upon those of the adults who raise and educate you. Beliefs are conditioned by the society and culture that surrounds you. Many times, these beliefs lend themselves to unfounded dogma and human propaganda. These types of beliefs can lead to irrational fears, for these irrational fears are based on the illusion of false belief systems. It is so important to examine your beliefs and ask yourself if there is not another way to examine life and the ideals you hold. If mankind can overcome his irrational fears, he will carve out a better life and future for all on the planet.

Fear that is justified is true fear surrounding a situation that would compromise a soul's safety or self preservation. You must determine the validity of this type of fear to determine your course of action or inaction as it pertains to the situation at hand. This type of fear would serve to assist in the decisions you would make about a situation that you might find yourself in. We would label this as a healthy fear, and you would be helped by tuning into the inner counsel that this would supply, and it would be the beneficial guidance tool.

This emotion would serve as safety and self preservation for the soul. A healthy fear would provide for your safety. If one had no fear of walking into a poisonous snake pit, one might walk into certain death. This is but one example of a healthy fear.

Your healthy fears are a protective device that are linked to mankind's instinct for survival. It is this fear that has aided mankind in his evolution. It is this fear that will aid you in times of your survival, for this fear can warn you of impending danger and cause your adrenalin to activate. When this fear is felt, it is important to activate. This is what is referred to as your fight or flight reaction. This is an important and healthy type of fear.

Examine your emotions, for they are the language of your soul. Make sure that you allow yourself a chance to listen to your inner voice of guidance as it pertains to your healthy fear. Fear has its place within your lives and if utilized properly, can be advantageous. We therefore, urge you to analyze your fears to determine their place and benefit within your lives.

Demna: The next emotion is.......

Anger

Anger is the expression of an unfulfilled soul and is an emotion of the low order. It is through anger that the soul allows itself to disengage from the Source.

When a soul's journey is not going as he would desire, much frustration and anger can result. Many of you know someone who is frustrated due to an unfulfilled life. These people tend to go through life without a hold on their reigns. Life is something that happens to them, and usually, the events that occur tend to be negative. This is mostly due to their lack of direction and belief in themselves. When lifetimes go sour, these people experience anger and frustration.

Mankind should realize that he is in control of his destiny, and his thoughts and beliefs determine the course of this destiny. Mankind can change his destiny by altering his belief system. There is no need for an unfulfilled life. There is no need for anger. Anger serves no benefits to anyone.

It is through anger that the seeds of hatred are sown just as the seeds of love are sown through joy. Anger and hatred are the polar opposites of joy and love. Anger is an emotion that can be, and will be, destructive if left to rule mankind. It is through hatred, as well as fear, that mankind has succeeded in destroying itself and many of its most treasured existence through many acts of destruction. Mankind must learn to overcome this very destructive emotion to ensure its evolution and life span on this planet that was given lovingly to mankind. If allowed to grow, this is the one emotion that will ensure the destruction of the human race.

Trying to eliminate anger is easier said than done, at times. Meditation and breathing deeply doesn't always seem to help. What advice do you have for those of us who are trying to work through our anger towards someone?

We would advise you to practice compassion and see the world view of the person you are angry with. Feel compassion for that person, for he may have caused your anger out of something as simple as his own fear of love.

It would be very difficult to feel compassion towards someone who has done something to greatly harm you or has committed a horrible crime towards you or someone you love. As an example, someone who may have committed a horrific crime like murdering someone you love. How can you feel compassion towards someone like this?

We realize this, and there are many times that healing can be attained through compassion and forgiveness. Compassion in this situation is very difficult for humans to feel, as well as forgiveness, but it is through compassion and forgiveness that your heart can begin to heal from such a tragedy. This is the reasoning behind some of the victim and perpetrator programs that exist. If compassion and forgiveness is withheld, it will ensure that the event will forever fester within your soul. It is quite possible that such an event may have occurred for the purpose of providing a lesson to you for this very reason, and by withholding compassion and forgiveness, the lesson may have been in vain. Remember that all these events are not random, and that there are lessons to be learned in every situation. There may have been a pre-existing agreement between these souls before they reincarnated into the specific reality, and that this agreement may have been for the purpose of mutual lessons.

This seems like such a cruel way to set up an event so that we can learn a life lesson.

Yes it does, but in the great scheme of reality, it is but a method that makes a necessary deep impact. World wars are cruel, but these also are considered agreements between victims and perpetrators.

When we are setting up these pre-existing agreements, aren't we considering how cruel and painful these lessons will be?

Some lessons are undertaken for the greater good of learning. Nothing is random, as we stated, and if all learning was to be one sided, it would not impart a proper lesson. Remember that even hatred has its place, for without hatred, you cannot fully appreciate love.

When you experience anger, you are throwing yourself out of alignment with the soul Source, and this is experienced by a feeling of being out of sorts, as you would term it. Anger serves no healthy purpose both physically and mentally, and it would not serve one to hold on to his anger. It will cause unease and disease if left unchecked and allowed to grow and fester. The best way to deal with and heal your anger, is through meditation and self realization that love is the true soul goal. Your best way to be, when confronted with anger, is to breathe deeply and meditate on your breath until you calm down.

Anger is a negative emotion and serves no unifying purpose for anyone involved. Instead, it will serve a destructive purpose and will lead to more anger and more negativity. If we examine the reasons for anger, we can begin to peel away the years and layers that have caused this build up of anger. Often times, anger is connected to our past experiences that have affected us adversely and that we have neglected to learn from. When these experiences brew without release or remedy, then a bitterness and anger will take root and grow within our souls. When we experience these situations without learning lessons from them, they become unresolved negative memories with no rhyme or reason. It is when we learn the lessons that these situations are brought into our lives to teach us, that we can experience great learning and great relief from these lessons.

Rather then let anger rule your life, determine the cause of this anger and allow yourself to release it and grow spiritually. If this anger is tied to your beliefs, then perhaps your beliefs are flawed and require re-examination. Be aware of which beliefs are perpetuating your anger, and be prepared to forgive these situations and to allow yourself to heal. Then you will be able to move away from anger, and towards joy.

Melanie: Your anger would be unnecessary if you lived your lives in light, and love, and compassion, for it is when we have love and compassion that we have understanding for each other, and our anger would dissipate. Your anger is unnecessary at times, for it is based on perceived injustices and not on truth. If you would turn to understanding in those times of anger, you could turn the anger into compassion and turn the compassion towards love. Your mind is capable of many beliefs that your brain perceives as truth. If you would look at your beliefs and turn them around, you could dissipate the anger around it and turn it around also.

Many times, your anger is based on an illusionary belief, for it is all an illusion. When we say that it is all an illusion, we mean that this reality is the illusion of our cooperative soul minds. We and our reality dwell within the Source mind.

Think of life as a play, and that you are all actors assuming a role. When the play is over, you shed these roles and assume your true selves. Such is the life and reality you live in. The people in your reality are all actors who share your play, and you create this illusion on a cooperative level. When your lives are over in your reality, you shed your bodies and go back to the Source.

If we can view reality in this way, then we can begin to see how our negative emotions are a result of our illusory beliefs. Your beliefs and perceptions are a part of this illusion that we talk about, and if you could begin to realize that this illusion is not as real as you believe, then it would help these emotions of negativity fall away, and they could be replaced by love and understanding. Your hatred is based on belief systems that are only real to you, and if you would shed them by disengaging yourself from your strong attachment to them, you would realize how your lives could be much happier.

How can you deal with anger, you may ask? Anger can be alleviated through understanding with, and of each other. If we can understand each other, we would not be so deeply affected by perceived injustices. Anger is alleviated through love, for if we loved our fellow beings, we would not commit acts of violence or injustice against each other. If we had compassion for each other, then we would not commit acts that would cause anger. Love, compassion, and understanding; this is the path to learning, and the path to mutual cooperation with each other. Melanie loves you all.

Em: Your love can dissipate anger. Try to get to the root and reasons for your anger, and try to work through it with love. If we remember that love will heal, then let love heal your anger. Remember that perception is important and that anger can be healed.

The next emotion is.......

Sorrow

Sorrow can best be described as sadness, and indicates a lack in one's life. If we are without love, we experience sorrow through a sense of disconnection and loss as a result. When the soul is not centered on its true course, we feel it throughout ourselves, and we feel a longing to be in the light of this true path. The sorrow felt, is the soul's reaction to this disconnection. When we have love, we have joy. When we lack love, we feel sorrow and loss of something dear. You must give love to receive love, for love generates love, bringing joy and abolishing sadness. Sadness or sorrow exists as a result of an unexpressed soul. When we are not on our true course, we feel unfulfilled and we feel this sense of lack which brings sorrow.

The concept is quite simple. Love begets love, and through love, all negativity is washed away. Try being negative when you are feeling love. It is impossible. Think of sorrow as the absence of love; and this is easily demonstrated when two people lose their love or when someone loses a loved one. The addition of love in one's life will truly alleviate sorrow. Mankind's true divinity is love, and when he truly discovers this, there will be no sorrow.

You say that sorrow is the result of the unexpressed soul. It is so hard for many of us on this planet to discover our passion and to live lives fully expressed. How can we accomplish this challenging task when there are so many hurdles in our paths, so that we may move away from sorrow and towards joy?

Life on your planet is for the purpose of rediscovering love through lessons learned, and sometimes to learn these lessons best, it is not always the easy route that must be chosen. The challenge is in learning the lesson and discovering the love and joy that exists as a result of the realization that the lesson imparts to us. In order to find love and joy, it will be discovered in the ability of the Source soul to overcome the hurdles presented. How wonderful do you feel when you have overcome an obstacle that has stood in your way? How joyful do you feel when you have reached the top of the mountain after a difficult climb? There would be very little joy to realize if everything came to you easily and effortlessly. There is no joy in anything attained without effort.

Your journey in this life is with purpose. When you are embarked on this journey and are on your true path, you will feel a sense of centeredness and joy. It is when you do not listen to your God Source and stray from your true path, that you feel a sense of sorrow. Meditation can help to re-center you so that you may vibrate like a tuned fork within the presence of the Source, where you will find your true joy. This will help to eliminate sorrow. Love will also eliminate sorrow. When you have lost love, you have lost joy and sense of purpose.

Make it a daily habit to allow love into your life, and make it a daily habit to share love with others, for it is through love that sorrow is healed. Love feeds the hungry. Love heals the sick. This is but a small example of how love alleviates sorrow. Mother Teresa is a good example of pure love and the service it provides for the needy. There are many people and organizations that devote themselves selflessly and lovingly to the service of providing for those less fortunate than themselves. True charity is an act of love. When we care for our fellow souls through love, compassion, and understanding, we are able to heal sorrow and bring joy. All misery can be healed if we truly love each other, for it is the absence of love that perpetuates sorrow.

Think of how you can help to alleviate sorrow, and make a step, no matter how small it may be, and you will discover that by healing someone else's sorrow, you will also heal yourself, and joy will take its place. Love will heal a broken heart no matter how broken it may be. Love is the path to joy, and love will be the path away from sorrow. Try to be understanding through your compassion for each other, for it will help you to understand the sorrow another feels, and let your heart heal the sorrow. There is no need for sorrow, as there is no need for emotions of the low order. If we could truly understand this, we could heal the planet in good time. Eliminate sorrow through love of one another, for we are all truly brethren.

Melanie: Always let love be your motivation, and joy will follow and sorrow will be eliminated. Make love your goal. Meditate daily, and this will be the case.

The next emotion is of the lowest order, and it must be discussed.

Hatred

Hatred is the darkest emotion we will experience in our lives, and it is so unnecessary, for truly it has no benefit whatsoever. Love is lost when hatred is expressed, and it will take us into the darkest places in our souls; and really this is sad, for there should be no darkness in the soul, for the soul is from the Source, and the Source is light and love.

When we have lost love, it is replaced by hatred, and hatred is the absence of love, compassion, understanding, and joy. When all of this is lost, we have hatred in its place. Hatred is the foundation where evil can flourish, and there is no sense in it. A soul who has lost love experiences anger and hatred in its place, and it is important to begin a healing through love, for love can heal hatred. A soul in despair can succumb to hatred as a result of un-fulfillment, and this can escalate to more hatred. This emotion can cause illness and disease within the person who holds the hatred. When we inflict hatred towards another, we become discordant within the Source. The Source loves us unconditionally no matter what harm we may inflict upon another, but we must ask you, do you love yourself? For if you loved yourself truly, then you would love one another as well. It is when we have hatred and loathing of ourselves, that we project this hatred onto others. We use the term "we" because hatred is noticed throughout the Source when it is expressed. This is not to mean that the Source feels hatred, but the Source notices all, including your hatred. Through free will, you continue to abuse each other through hatred, but remember that this will affect you as well, for what we give, we also receive, and what we project onto others will also affect us.

What should we do when we come across a person who is filled with hatred? Is it best to avoid a person like this altogether?

No. Everyone we meet has a lesson to teach us, and if we avoid these lessons, we will simply revisit them at another time. The best way to deal with hatred is to show love and compassion, for hatred is the result of love unfulfilled, and it is through love that hatred can be absolved. Do not confront hatred with hatred, for the results are always devastating. Hatred does not resolve hatred, and the attempt is always futile. Love is the quest, and love is also the quest for the hateful person. Woe is the life of the hateful person, for this person knows not the results and peace of soul that love brings.

You say that we shouldn't go out of our way to avoid these people, but isn't it important to surround ourselves with positive people?

Yes it is, but we must also remind you that every situation is a chance for learning. If people would apply love and compassion to their day to day living and situations, there would be no hatred, for hatred would be absolved. If nations that hated each other ignored and avoided each other, there would be no resolve, but in fact, eventually this hatred would lead to disagreements through misunderstanding and also, possibly, war. If nations that hated each other would instead, come together in compassion, they could then find in themselves the ability to love and understand each other, thus resolving their hatred and differences. By avoiding each other's hatred, we do not resolve anything.

How is it possible that what we project onto others, will also affect us?

Because the law of attraction, which we term magnetism, makes it thus. What we send forth in energy also attracts like energy to us. If we send forth hatred, the energy that is hatred will also be attracted to this energy. Like attracts like. Love attracts love. Hate attracts hate.

There are many people who don't love themselves. How can we begin to love ourselves so that we can begin to eliminate hatred from our lives? Sometimes hatred is so deeply rooted within the human psyche that it seems like a daunting task.

Yes, and this is one of the most daunting tasks that the human race has, for it seems easier to love others than it is to love yourselves, but remember this; to truly love another, you must love yourself, for if not, then love towards another is misguided. If you do not love yourself first, it is not possible to truly love another without experiencing a total breakdown eventually, in the love towards another. Sometimes, when we do not love ourselves first, we seek to validate ourselves through someone else's love. You cannot validate yourself through anyone but yourself and your true connection to the Source. It is through this connection to the Source that you can heal yourself and discover true pure love. If you could gain an understanding of the Source's love, then loving yourself would come more naturally, and loving others would be a deeper and purer experience.

False belief systems foster hatred. Beliefs about prejudice towards one another, fear of one another, and all these beliefs cause hatred to rise within you. Fear of each other's beliefs around religion have caused hatred. All these things that cause hatred are through lack of compassion and understanding for each other's beliefs.

Many people have hatred towards each other based on race and religion. At times this hatred has led to violence towards one another. What can we do to eliminate this from our lives and planet?

We would advise you to realize that you are all Source soul brothers and sisters with a common bond and common lessons through different or mutual experiences in your journeys through life. It would be advisable to remember that you all share many of the same fears, and loves, and challenges. We have answered this question in other ways, but it is never wrong to repeat that you are all brethren, and inside your many different colored skins and religions, you are all a part of that one Source who birthed you. You are all one within the many colors you inhabit.

If you allowed each other free true expression, you would discover there is no need to fear and hate what you do not understand, for each one of you is on his own journey in this life, and each one of you is here to learn and grow within the Earth experience. If you could understand this, you would freely allow others their journeys without fear and hatred of what you do not understand. It is lack of knowledge and fear of the unknown that fosters distrust and leads to hatred.

On the one hand, I am in total agreement, but I would have a hard time with this if allowing people their journeys means allowing people to murder, to start wars, to try to repress people's civil liberties, and so forth.

Someone who is not allowing another his civil liberties, defeats the purpose of what we say because to allow someone his journey would be without interference of his civil liberties. By allowing others their journeys, we speak of religious freedom without fear, we speak of the diversity of practicing your culture without intrusion, we speak of allowing others the right to be themselves without imposing your beliefs upon them. When you speak of murderers, you miss our point, for does not the murderer impose himself on another's journey? The act of murder disrupts another's journey in life. We speak of allowing each other the right to exist without imposing your will upon them. Your wars and arguments would not exist if you would allow each other to rightfully exist. Let them be.

Hatred can be best described as an intense dislike, often without true basis or understanding. An intense dislike that has no reason is very dangerous indeed. You are experiencing wars and murders as a result of hatred without foundation. This causes much pain and suffering that is needless. Hatred is the absolute absence of love, and love is the cure for hatred. Try to love each other, and try to understand each other, and try to allow each other growth and lessons in their journeys, without fear.

Hatred is also the result of an unfulfilled soul. When you are unfulfilled, you become angry, and this anger can lead to jealousy and hatred towards others who represent fulfillment to you. You begin to hate that which you cannot have. You begin to hate that which you covet because you cannot have it. Realize that you cannot have it because you lack belief that you can acquire a thing. Belief is important, and we have discussed this with you. If you examine your belief systems, you will begin to see that you alone are responsible for everything you have or lack in your life. You alone are the captain of your ship, and you alone steer the tiller.

Hatred is unnecessary, and it does not belong in your world if you do not want it. Hatred can be resolved, and the resolution of this low emotion will herald a greater era into your world. We would urge you all to undergo this evolution and discover your true essence.

Love is the remedy for hatred, and it will overcome many emotions of the low order. Love is the emotion that heals all emotions of the low order. Focus on love, and hate will dissipate. Hatred will destroy. Love will build.

You say love is the remedy for hatred, but this sounds so simplistic. How does this work, and how do we make this work to eliminate hatred in the world? I can feel all the love I would like, but I can't see this eliminating hatred in the world.

We would advise that many of you come together for a common purpose of peace, love, and healing. There is much hatred in your world between countries and races, and this is due to past injustices that have occurred. It is important to come together as a common humanity that shares this planet, and to have compassion and understanding for each other's differences and cultures and beliefs. Do not force your beliefs on one another, for you are all here in your various races and religions for your own learning opportunities. Allow each other the right to exist, and allow each other to practice your beliefs and religions unencumbered, for when we allow each other to live and let live, we can begin to wash away hatred and to begin to heal our differences. We are all on the same journey, but we are simply choosing to utilize different methods to learn the same lessons. Come together as a family, a neighborhood, a county, a country, and a planet. In this way, you can absolve and eliminate hatred and allow true love to fill the void.

Em: Be kind to all, for it will come back to you. Em and Melanie love you.

This will end our chapter on emotions. The next chapter is to be titled.......

Chapter Ten:

Reality

Em: Reality is but an illusion of collusion. We are all participants in the reality that we dwell in. We will focus primarily on the reality that you currently dwell in. We say currently because this is not the only reality that exists. It is one of many, and it is one of many that you have experienced.

The current reality that you exist in is one that you all participate in the creation of. It has rules of engagement, per se, and these rules lay the foundation of the parameters that you operate within. It has been created as a playing field, per se, so that we may experience life and learning from a unique perspective. The Source, in an attempt to understand itself, had to devise a method of comparison and experience for self-actualization. If you don't experience sadness, how can you know joy? If you don't experience hatred, how can you know love?

I thought that our reality was created so that we could learn lessons, and understand and experience who and what we are, but here you say that the Source had to devise a method of comparison and experience for self-actualization. Doesn't the Source already know who it is?

Yes, but the Source existed as a singular, and as a singular it experienced only that everlasting singularity of now. It also wanted to experience plurality, and in order to do so, it established many levels that it could experience in order to achieve comparison within itself. It sent forth Source souls as a parent sends forth children because this was a method of experience.

Can you explain what you mean by singularity?

By singularity, we mean that the Source existed as one lonely entity, as you would put it. Imagine if you were the only human on your planet and that this planet only encompassed the space that you occupied, then you would begin to understand that your concept of being would be limited to your direct experience and perception of this existence. You would long for love and companionship of others, and you would long for the expansion of your world and experience. As a singularity, the Source simply was, and all of what it was, was loving conscious energy. The Source wanted to know itself and all of what it could be. The Source wanted to multiply itself to share all of what it could be. This desire, in and of itself, created the explosion of all souls and possibilities. Thus were Source souls birthed, and thus were all Universes and levels of reality birthed. This is ever expanding as the creation of worlds and levels of realities continue to be birthed. By birthing all that exists, the Source can compare all experiences and realities against itself. All That Is reflects itself unto itself through the experiences of its Source souls. If mankind could understand this concept, he can begin to realize how the Source began to expand its reality through unconditional love, and therefore, birthed an entire Universe and gave birth to its Source souls. It is through this love and yearning that we can owe all of our lives and experiences to.

How is it that this Source came into existence in the first place?

This is a question that many have asked, and we admit that it is quite mind boggling to many, but the Source existed as a unit of conscious awareness in a space unhampered by any laws of any dimensions, and although it is difficult to explain in Earthly terms, we will attempt to do just that.

Imagine the moment of an everlasting now, and imagine that this moment is occupied by self awareness, and imagine that this self awareness has a longing to expand. It is through the longing and awareness that makes it expand, and as this awareness expands, it grows to encompass greater awareness, greater love, and greater joy. Imagine that this is the genie that left the bottle and through greater love and awareness, can never be a singularity again, and this is why it continues to grow forever in the everlasting now.

But where did this unit of conscious awareness come from? How did it begin?

The Source has no beginning and no end. It simply was and is. The human mind cannot comprehend this concept because your linear time dictates that everything has a beginning and an ending. These are simply the rules of engagement for your reality.

In the previous chapter, you stated that hatred is unnecessary, so how is it that hatred exists in our reality?

Hatred is unnecessary if you would accept unconditional love, but since many are still striving to achieve and experience unconditional love, hatred has its place as a tool of learning and comparison. In the last chapter, we spoke of hatred as being an emotion of the lowest order, but even hatred has its place in the stage of reality in relation to the self-actualization of the Source souls, so you see, it is all relative and interconnected. Hatred will no longer have a home on your planet once all of mankind has reached its ultimate goal of unconditional love.

The Earth was created within the Source mind as a place for the Source souls to inhabit as they learned their lessons and grew towards self-knowledge and actualization. The three dimensional rules of your reality were put in place as a general guideline to operate within. It is as a sports game has rules to follow so the game can maintain a sense of logic. We say a sense because beneath the surface of reality is the sub world, per se, that supports it.

What do you mean by this? Can you explain this sub world?

It makes your world exist, for *without* the sub-world, your world would not exist. The sub-world is the world of atoms, and cells, and molecules that comprise all that exists within your world. Energy then animates and powers everything, breathing life into all that exists.

Your reality has existed for millions, and more, of your Earth years. We spoke previously, of the Universe's birthing of your planet and its preparation for the emergence of the human race. It did not happen over night, as you would say, although in our dimension, there is no passage of time, and all exists in an everlasting now. Many eons of your time passed before your emergence, and the souls who were to inhabit your reality waited with excitement for this time to come, and it was an event that we all looked forward to.

You say that the birthing of our planet and the emergence of our souls onto this plane was an exciting event that we all looked forward to. There are many other planets in the Universe. What makes planet Earth so special?

Love, in its many forms and variations, is what makes your planet so special. It is a unique multidimensional experiment that does not exist elsewhere. Planet Earth is the

Garden of Eden of which your bible speaks, and this is why we lament the pollution and disruption that mankind is inflicting upon Eden. Planet Earth is special in its unique way, as we said because everything is a reflection of God's love. Children are the reflection of love in all species, as they symbolize the creation of life and love. Each new season brings the birth of life, and each procreation, whether plant, or animal, or human, symbolizes the new dawning of life. Earth has given mankind many comparisons of love and beauty, and this exists nowhere else in the Universe. It is a unique experiment in the creation of love and beauty.

Each world has its parameters of operation. Some operate on pure intellect only while others operate on emotion. Planet Earth encompasses all that it can be. Intellect, artists, scientists; there are many colors in the spectrum of Earthly experience. This covers humans, but you also have many species within each grouping. You have many races of humans, many species of animals, many species of flowers, and so forth. Planet Earth encompasses many probabilities whereas other planets are limited in their forms and experiences.

You are all a part of an exciting master plan of three dimensional reality. It is a grand plan of genius, and we are all genius God Source souls who have the privilege of participation and grand learning opportunity. If you could see what we see, you would be truly amazed at the perfection of this plan of learning, and growth, and self-actualization of the Source souls. All of us have a part in reality, even those of us who are not directly inhabiting the Earth in three dimensional form. There is a cooperation between our level of reality and yours, that you are not even aware of. We have all participated in the exciting reality that plays out on planet Earth.

What can you tell us about the cooperation between your level of reality and ours? How do we all participate in the reality that plays out on our planet?

We all are co-creators of our realities, and the cooperation that exists between us is one of co-creators on planet Earth. We were all involved in the co-creation of the reality that we live, as well as all of the developments and strides that have been undertaken since the beginning of your Earth time. The inventions that have taken place are cooperative ventures between our two realities. We are not as removed as you may think we are, and we have a level of communication with mankind that is subtle, yet profound. Many of the revolutionary ideas that come to you are supplied by us through instinct or what you term inspiration. We are in constant communication with mankind, but you do not hear us yet, for your third eye is yet to open.

If we could see what you see, what would we see?

If mankind could see what we see, you would see the depth of beauty, and colors, and sounds that bring joy to all of existence within the mind of God. You would see mansions like no other. You would see the beauty of the Universe in all of its splendor, and color, and explosion of life. You would see all the spirits and lives that are, and ever will be. You would see dimensions that your scientists can only hypothesize, and much, much more. Life that the Source has given us all, is the greatest gift that could possibly be, and then God outdoes himself by giving us multitudes of splendors for our enjoyment.

Does our reality exist in the Source's mind? Are we all just illusions that play out scenes in the Source's imagination?

In a manner of speaking, yes. We exist in the Source's mind because the Source is everywhere and everything; therefore, everything that exists, exists within the Source. Illusions are not real if mankind believes thusly, however, illusions within the Source's mind have a reality that is governed by each dimension; therefore, it is very real to all within each dimension. Think of it as a stage play or film. Mankind must realize that the illusions we speak of are the stage plays that each Source soul agrees to play out in each dimension. The play is make believe; therefore, one could argue that it is not real, but the actors within the play are all experiencing a real event as they participate in the play. Experience is quite real, and mankind's experience is very real, even though each Source soul is agreeing to play its part. In this manner, so is all of reality an illusion, but a real event for all concerned. It is all an illusion that is co-created by all of life within the Source, but it is very real. All that you think becomes real in your world when you breathe life into it. Such is the Source.

When this planet was in its infancy, it went through many levels of reality before humans inhabited it. This was all in preparation for the experience of humanity that you now know. The dinosaur age was an experimental phase that Earth went through in order to establish ground rules for your existence. All animals are a part of the Source, and they too, have a part to play in the Source's self-actualization. This is best expressed as the Source learning base emotions and instincts without the genius of human thought. This experience laid the ground work for the Source to understand instincts of mammals, of which you are an offshoot. Before we added conscious thought, we experimented with pure emotion and instinct only, so you see, this was the foundation that came before conscious thought and intelligence was added to the mix. As a result, it is only logical that the dinosaur age would have an expiry date. This was also our experiment with form. Which form would best serve the Source's purpose? At first, as we stated, the Source needed to perform a test drive as you would term it.

Em will try to explain in human terms of understanding, the evolution of your world.

Once the Source had experienced knowledge and self-actualization on a base level, as you would term it, the Source was ready to evolve to the next level. In order to achieve the next level, the Earth needed to ready itself. The dinosaurs could not exist along with humans, for humans would become extinct themselves as a result, for dinosaurs were operating on pure emotion and instinct for survival and growth. They would simply have been the bully on the block, and you would have perished.

The solution was to start anew with a fresh course. The incident that cleaned this slate was a planned event put into action by the cooperative God and soul Source. You are a result of that natural evolution, and it is not over yet. God has a master plan, as you would term it.

What can you tell us about the incident that cleaned the slate of dinosaurs from this planet?

It is as your scientists suspect. There was indeed an asteroid that broke through your atmosphere and did not fully disintegrate before hitting Earth, due to its great size. This event caused a great misplacement of your seas and oceans, causing many great tidal waves. It affected the Earth to a degree that caused eruptions, and caused displacement of species, and great loss of life. The skies darkened and much debris fell on the planet, causing a shift in weather patterns and causing changes in temperatures. The ensuing result was a loss of sunshine and rays infiltrating the planet. This loss of sun and rays caused the plant life to virtually disappear. It affected the food chain, and many species who survived the initial impact perished in the ensuing changes that resulted. This cleanse was necessary because the Source was ready to experience the next level. There were some species that survived, and they are a big change from what used to be. These surviving examples of the dinosaur age have been experiencing a world that is drastically different from whence they came. The world today is much different than the one they evolved from.

The next step for the Source was the natural evolution from emotion and instinct, to conscious thought, and this precipitated the evolution of mankind on this planet, and this planet is very unique and special indeed, for it is one of the

Source's greatest experiments, and we are all so fortunate to be active participants and co-creators with God, for we are truly in partnership with the God Source.

When the Earth was cleansed of dinosaurs, there were some forms that evolved and survived, but not all were chosen for survival. Why did some survive and not others, you may ask. This was primarily as a tool of measure to see where we came from and how far we have progressed. An example of this measuring tool is the reptilian alligator. By observing the alligator, we have insight into the pure emotion and instinct of where our reality has started. This is a measuring tool that allows us to chart our progress.

As we continue to evolve, we will be further amazed as we continue to measure this progress against those animals that have walked with us since the beginning of our time, as we know it.

You stated that our natural evolution is not over yet, and that God has a master plan. What is God's master plan?

We are Source.

Before you answer our question, can you tell us a little more about who you are?

We are from a level beyond your guides. We have never incarnated. We are of the Source. We serve the Source.

How do you serve the Source?

We serve the Source by doing what is required to ensure balance of his creation and to ensure that all his creation be in a state of unity throughout. We are teachers of higher planes and messengers of higher planes. There are those Source souls who have never incarnated, but whose purpose is to oversee all creation. We ensure the harmonious balance of All That Is. In mankind's terminology, he may utilize the term angels for us, for indeed we are angels of the Source, and in times of imminent imbalance or need, we will appear to assist balances where needed. In mankind's terms, balances are referred to as situations of great need. We have appeared as, what mankind refers to as, good Samaritans in times of great need. We appear as human and disappear without notice when we have accomplished our task.

Make all of your lessons on Earth worthwhile for the learning of your soul's, and spiritual, growth. Your purpose is to find your Source through integration and ascension. Mankind will one day evolve beyond the need for his physical body. It will be as if you are inhabiting planet Earth without the need of physical vehicles. The third eye that you seek to open is but the beginning.

What makes this planet one of the Source's greatest experiments?

Melanie: It is as we said. Planet Earth is Eden, and it has many life forms who represent God's experience in one place. It, in a sense, is the physical representation of the Source. It has beautiful vistas. It has beautiful creatures who express divine creation through their mere existence. There are many avenues of cultures, and religions, and beliefs, all for the Source's purpose of self-actualization. It is a very unique creation. It has such a diversity to honor the love of the Source.

You say that the time is approaching for us to begin to understand the master plan. Why is now the time? What is so special about the approaching time?

Mankind's growth is accelerating, and it is a natural part of his evolution. It is the era of progress and development like none other that has existed. It is the natural step towards the spiritual development of mankind and the opening of his third eye. The time is here for the beginning of an internal shift and a step towards spiritual development. There are some who do not comprehend this and live in a closed reality because they are governed only by what they can see, and sense, and think in Earthly rational terms about, but this must change. Some of mankind is closed to the possibility that other alternatives exist beyond the physical world they see and experience, and part of this reason is their strong attachment to the physical and to things that are coveted as opposed to the spiritual richness that exists within mankind. There are, however, those of you who are aware in the greater sense of the word and whose journey towards the spiritual realm has already been underway. Those of you who have begun this journey, will be the pioneers of a much braver new world. Yes, there are many messengers among you whose purpose it is to lead this pilgrimage.

Many of you are messengers, as we have said, and the time is approaching for you to begin to understand the master plan. We will talk through you and attempt to open the third eye of humanity, but this lesson in reality is but a beginning.

Em: You have been making plans for this reality since the beginning of time, as you term it. When the time was right and the Earth was ready, man began to evolve. We spoke of the dinosaur age as an experiment in emotion and instinct. When the Source souls ended this phase, we began to inhabit early man in an attempt to evolve the intelligence of our three dimensional awareness. As mankind evolved, we evolved through the growth of our senses and intelligence.

Mankind's evolution has been premeditated, and all of evolution is premeditated. Time is a factor on Earth, and it is because of time that evolution has taken millions of years. Man is the vehicle in which the Source is experiencing itself through, in an effort to attain self-actualization. It is a stepping stone of the grand master plan, and one day evolution will evolve to such a level that you cannot yet fathom, but we are getting ahead of ourselves once more.

How did man first appear on Earth? Where did we come from?

Mankind began as a thought in the Source's mind, just as the Universe began as a thought in the Source's mind. When the Source first thought of creating the Universe of experience, there occurred, what you term as, the big bang. It was suddenly thought into an explosion of reality. When the Earth was ready, the Source began to experience the realities that exist on your planet. When the Source thought of mankind, the Source souls left the Source in an explosion that sent forth many of these Source soul seeds, and they gravitated towards planet Earth. At first, they inhabited Earth as souls and did not occupy mass. As they continued to experience the Earth through inhabiting it as souls, they became attached to the planet, and as a result of Earth's gravitational pull, their vibrations became denser, and through this continued dense vibration, they were caused to become dense themselves until they discovered that they were locked inside their physical bodies. Thus began mankind's dense existence on this planet, and through repeated life journeys, you are experiencing reality as a part of the Source's self-actualization, and through your continued evolution, are finding your way back to the higher vibrations that were once the norm for you.

Was it by accident that we became locked inside our physical bodies?

Nothing is random. We are on the journey of experience on behalf of the Source. It is a part of the journey of the Source's self-actualization. In the beginning of mankind's existence on Earth, he was a more spiritual being and could leave his body at will. As time progressed, his nature changed, and as a result, he became locked within his form. During the evolution of your planet, it has been occupied by many forms of experiment and experience. We spoke of the dinosaurs as one of these forms. Mankind is the form that best represents the awareness and intelligence of the Source, although mankind is still limited in his scope. All life began from the Source. Mankind has yet to reach his full potential. Mankind is still evolving.

But where did our bodies come from?

Your bodies were created from the same substance of the Earth, and they are a reflection of your planet's substance. As mankind evolved, his features evolved into the human you know today. You are wondering about the evolution of a single living cell that would multiply itself into eventual form. Yes, this is how some of your species evolved, and this has taken billions of your Earth years, but this is not how all species evolved. Remember that you are dealing with a God Source whose thoughts become things of a concrete nature, and as a result, not all has to develop along the lines that you are accustomed to. Mankind came to be through the thought of God.

Why is the vehicle of man a stepping stone of the grand master plan?

Because it became dense through lowered vibrations, and the experience of this density will eventually lead us through a path of spirituality that will raise the vibrations of mankind to the level of higher frequency, thus eliminating the need for dense bodies. It is through the vehicle of having a dense body that mankind is learning to raise his vibration to the point of discarding his density. His journey is a means of regaining his higher vibration once more, thus ascending once again into spirit. In reaching this level, mankind will learn the value of his connection to the Source.

How are we a reflection of God?

We make ourselves a reflection of God by being creators on our own world, and we are a reflection of God, for we reflect back to God what God has created.

Man is the vehicle as a car is a vehicle for you, and through the evolution of mechanics, you have created greater vehicles than you once imagined possible. Such is mankind. Back to reality.

Through planned evolution, you have grown in many aspects that reflect the aspects of the soul at the Source level. It is a microcosm of a macrocosm; mankind being the microcosm and the Source being the macrocosm. One is a reflection of the other. Reality is planned right down to the finest detail, and though you may not realize it, you are planning every aspect of your life, whether it be through subconscious or conscious thought.

When mankind evolved, the Source had another method of creating reality and experience. It was on a dimensional plane as opposed to a spiritual plane, although a spiritual level coexists within mankind as mankind exists within the spiritual level. God's greatest experiment is through you.

As we evolved, we began to realize our dreams and turn them into reality. The necessity that we experienced on many levels through our journeys caused us to create our reality as these necessities arose. Hunger caused us to create tools for hunting, and the need for traveling caused the invention of the wheel. In this manner has mankind evolved to his present state. He had many needs as he evolved; and when we speak of "he", we are speaking of ourselves as the Source souls who inhabited the vehicle of mankind. These needs caused the evolution of mankind. As intelligence grew and required a larger brain, man grew to accommodate the necessities that were required of the human body. What does this have to do with reality? For this chapter reads more like a chapter on evolution. Evolution and reality are intertwined because without the reality we created, evolution would have been impossible. You see, it was through evolution that man created reality, and through reality that evolution was brought into existence.

Mankind created his reality through his connection with the Source and through the Source's desire for experience, and self-actualization, and knowledge. Mankind has been a vehicle driven by the Source in an attempt to grow and expand in the Universe of experience within the Universe of the Source mind. Through the manipulation of reality, through the conscious needs of man as he evolved, the Source has expanded. The reality man created was necessary to experience his evolution, and it has been slow in your terms, but was necessary at the time because baby steps were being taken. You may notice that due to man's current intelligence, evolution is speeding up. The manner that man invented necessities to survive and grow has also been useful for you now, for as your archeologists look back, you can piece together your journey and learn from it.

Mankind is experiencing a growth in technology, and concepts, and modernization. This is leading to an expanded awareness that is connected to the acquisition of knowledge. As a result, it accelerates his knowledge and spirituality in general.

Melanie: Reality has been a slow process for the evolution of mankind, and this is because the Source souls had started their experience through animals in order to gain knowledge through emotions and instinct, as we mentioned. When this phase ended, we began a new phase as we journeyed through evolution and mankind in an effort to move from emotions and instinct towards self realization, self consciousness, and intelligence. It is through the desire of the Source that this journey has been possible, and it is through the love of the Source that each Source soul has retained his own identity and free will, for the Source so loves us that it is willing to allow us to retain this separate identity, even through integration with the Source. In other words, when we experience a physical death, we retain our own identities and merge with the Source at the same time. It is like having an identity within an identity. Two for the price of one, as you would term it.

Mankind's evolution has been planned, and though it may not seem so at times, we all create our own realities through our thoughts and intentions. In this way, mankind has also created the reality of evolution through each individual's thoughts, dreams, and intentions. Though it may not seem so to you, we all have a part to play in this and we all manipulate our own realities. If you would grasp this concept, you would be able to create a better reality for yourselves, and many stumbling blocks would be eliminated because you would realize that stumbling blocks are created by your own fears. Once you banish these fears and replace them with your goals and desires, you will begin to create the realities that you would prefer for yourselves.

Mankind, in his evolution, had a purer thought pattern than you do now, for evolutionary man had to create his reality through his necessities, and his fears could have literally killed him or caused your extinction. Evolutionary man is a beacon of enlightenment and a testament to fearlessness and growth for all of humanity today. He is an ancestor that you can be proud of, for he truly birthed your nation and world today. It is through evolutionary man, that you all owe your lives and current reality to, for through his courage and manipulation of reality, you have survived.

Evolutionary man operated his reality on a purer level than many of you do today. His limited intelligence caused him to operate on a survival and growth mode, and there was no room for fear of what might be except for the caution he had towards the elements and predators. But in this caution there existed a respect for these two elements, for in respecting them, he could learn to deal with them. Fear would have contributed to his demise. He had to put fear aside and learn to overcome and deal with these elements. This made him a better hunter, a better tool maker, and a better inventor, generally. You see, fear, or rather a respect of the challenges, is a great motivator for evolution and growth. Mankind's manipulation of reality has brought you to this present day, and it is important to understand how reality operates so that you can best operate within reality.

Make sure that you use meditation as a tool to operate your reality and to help achieve the goals you have. We have spoken about meditation and belief systems. These all play a part in helping to operate your reality to your benefit and to the benefit of modern man. In turn this benefits the Source souls and the Source in its continuing growth towards self-actualization, and knowledge, and experience.

When you begin to manipulate your reality, you will ease up on your fears, and your reality will occur more easily. Mankind is going through a growth, and we are here to help facilitate this growth through many messengers such as these we currently communicate through. Part of this growth entails a greater understanding of reality and how to manipulate it for the greater good of mankind, the animals, and the planet itself. You are going through a growth that is unprecedented in history, and it is important to understand reality and to become a peaceful, unified world.

When you can begin to understand this and to operate reality, you will go through your next growth phase. Do not let your fears control you. Do not let your fears create hatred, for this will stunt your growth and will slow the process and even retard your growth which is so necessary for your continuing evolution. Your legend is yet to be fulfilled.

Melanie: Many of you are now wondering how to manipulate reality. That is why the next chapter is titled.......

Reality

Chapter Eleven:

Magnetism: The Law of Attraction

Melanie: Magnetic energy is the basis of all spiritual energy, and it is available to all of us. We will explain what magnetism is in spiritual terms and explain how to use it.

You are all powered by spirit, and without spirit your body is but an organic shell, and this organic shell requires the energy of spirit to animate it and to keep it from decaying. The life it has is life force supplied by spirit, and because of spirit, it can operate within this dimension as ruled by its laws. In the spirit level, there is no requirement for such a vehicle because this level is ethereal and not organic. The reality you dwell in is a reality of mass, space, time, and volume. In order for spirit to operate within this reality, it must occupy three dimensional form and mass. Without it, we cannot be seen or operate within its laws. Other realities have their own laws of operation, and in order for spirit to occupy them, we must do so under their laws.

Because we are both spirit and mass, does this mean that we operate under two separate laws; three dimensional law and spiritual law?

Make sure that you understand the difference between mass that is inanimate and mass that is animated by the spirit of the Source, such as yourself. We mentioned that mankind is but a vehicle that the spirit uses to navigate in the three dimensional plane that you inhabit, but that this dimension has rules of engagement that the spirit utilizes with which to navigate while operating on this plane. Yes, you are spirit, but you are spirit that is inhabiting an organic vehicle at this time. When magnetism is utilized by the spirit that inhabits your organic vehicle, it must acquiesce to the laws of your dimension. When you vacate your organic vehicle, you reenter the world of pure spirit where we currently reside. Once you are in this realm of pure spirit, then laws change accordingly to adapt to this environment. Mankind is but the vehicle for spirit. It is but the car you drive in your current world and is not to be confused with the real you.

As spirit form, how are you able to operate in three dimensional law when you appear to us physically?

We are not governed by your laws of reality, and can, therefore, manipulate them at will. We are able to enter your dimension at will, but this does not mean that we do so by assuming physical mass, although at times we have done so due to specific circumstances. We are able to manipulate physical objects through the use of the Universal energy of magnetism. We have at times materialized physical objects, but again this is due to specific circumstances. It is not a common occurrence, but the times are chosen discriminately.

So you are saying that you can manipulate physical matter as well?

Yes, if we so choose, but we do so discriminately.

You have created this reality en masse. We have created this reality en masse. We, as spirit, are an energy life form, as you would term it, and as energy we cannot die, but we can be transformed through will. We are a conscious, loving energy form that is self-aware, and all knowing.

You state that magnetism is the law of attraction. How would you define the law of attraction?

Quite simply, the law of attraction dictates that what you focus on, you will attract. Magnetism is the energy of attraction, and we are all infused with it. All of us are capable of attracting energy or repelling energy, and we can control it at will. All of you who dwell in three dimensional form also have the power of magnetism at your disposal. The difference is that we, in spirit form, can use this magnetism to attract instantaneously, and you, in Earthly form, have the laws of time and space as a factor. We, in spirit form, are aware of this energy and have knowledge of how to utilize it. Humans are learning to use it and are also in the process of its discovery. Magnetism, or the law of attraction, as many of you term it, works somewhat like the magnets that you are familiar with. Magnetism is, simply, the law of attraction, and this law permeates the Universe and the Source. Magnetism is a powerful source of energy, and your evolution will expand as you become more familiar with it. It can be a great source of energy and power for your civilization, and love must be a part of this equation. All of you possess this power, but are still blind as to how to use it, and to its existence within you as a life force, and as a power source to attract and mold your reality.

Can you explain what you mean by this last sentence? You say we are still blind in knowing how to use magnetism.

Magnetism is an energy that has always existed, and mankind is in the process of understanding it. Although you are aware of energy and understand its use in conductors such as batteries, your civilization has yet to fully grasp how it applies to the human body and to the spiritual entity that resides within that body. When mankind opens his third eye, he will gain a better understanding of All That Is and how it all is.

All of you can use the energy of magnetism to create the reality that you want to attract into your lives. Thoughts have energy, and words have energy. These words and thoughts either attract or repel, just as a magnet does. If you focus on something, your focus will attract it towards you just as if you were a magnet.

Have you noticed how negative people always seem to have negative circumstances in their lives? This is their frame of mind and thought that attracts these situations to them. If you focus on things long enough, the Universe will conspire to supply them to you, and what you focus on, you will attract. When you want to change your life, you must change your mind because this is where your reality stems from, and this is where the changes must begin. It is through thought and magnetism that reality can be shaped, and we are all capable of these changes.

The energy that powers your body is the same energy that shapes your reality. This energy is the soul Source energy, and it is pure in its soul state, but in human form, this energy is controlled, at times, by the human ego and all its beliefs and fears. Mankind has a challenge in his form that is not experienced in the spirit state, but mankind can overcome this hurdle, and we will attempt to show you how.

Meditation will help to utilize magnetism to your advantage and it will help you to gain control of this energy and to manipulate it. All your magnetic energy comes from the Source, and by connecting with the Source, you can learn to utilize it for your greater good. Meditate, as instructed in chapter one, and utilize the method in the belief chapter to focus on altering your reality through changing your belief system.

If you want to attract something into your life, you must alter the belief you have towards it. If you have limiting beliefs about the reality you want to attract, then you will attract the limitations that you hold. What you focus on, you will get. If you want to attract a job, but feel you have no qualifications, you will not magnetize it towards you. If, on the other hand, you realize that in order to have the job of your dreams you need to have the education first, then the best approach would be to attract the school of your dreams. In *your* reality, the horse must still come before the cart. Logic dictates that the knowledge should be in place first. You cannot focus on being a real estate agent if you don't know the first thing about selling houses. Meditate, instead, on attracting the right school or course to manifest itself to you. In this manner, you can begin to set a course in motion that will lead you to your dream. Meditation and beliefs are the keys to attracting your desires into your life.

In the chapter on belief systems, you spoke of elements being broken down to their tiniest levels, leaving us with pure energy. Just to make sure we're clear on this; everything that exists is made of pure energy. Our thoughts are also pure energy. This energy is magnetic, and its magnetic nature is of such that it attracts like minded energy. This like minded energy can be in the form of people, events, and, or material things. It is our thoughts, and especially our beliefs, that determine that which we will attract or materialize in our lives.

This that we speak of is what you term as the law of attraction. It is the Universal law. The energy is Source energy which creates, inhabits, and powers everything, right down to the smallest molecule, cell, atom, and so forth. Magnetism, as we said, is the law of attraction and this is an example of it. Make sure that you meditate on that which you would like to attract, and if magnetism is pure, it will attract that which you desire. By magnetism being pure, we mean that you should focus on what you want, not what you don't want. Everything is energy. When you break down any element to its most finite point, what you get is the energy of All That Is, which either creates or animates any being in reality, as you know it. Without energy, your thought cannot exist, as without air you cannot breathe.

Make sure that your thoughts are true. If you tell yourself that you want to become a real estate agent, but you lack conviction and belief in your abilities, then the magnetism will not attract it, for you will attract what you focus on. If you tell yourself that you don't want to get fat, then what you are really focusing on is getting fat. Instead, you should focus on becoming thin. Replace the thought of getting fat with the thought of becoming slim. This is how reality works, and this is how reality is formed. You get what you focus on, even if what you're focusing on is something that you do not want.

Em: Reality is easier to manipulate than you believe, for it always conspires to materialize for you, for this is how magnetism works. Make sure that your thoughts are pure. By this, we mean that you should cast all doubts aside when you try to manipulate your desired reality into existence. Your doubts will become impediments and the reality that you desire will be thwarted. Do not focus on what you don't want, but focus on what you want and start taking steps towards its materialization. Trust that the soul Source is conspiring to make your desires materialize. Trust the process and be open to receiving what the Source is sending your way, even though it may not make sense at the time.

Sometimes in order to receive your desired reality, other events must transpire first because these events may lead you to your desire. Do not turn a blind eye to what the Source is sending you. If you want to become a real estate agent, the Universe may send you an advertisement for a course relating to your desired vocation. In this manner, the Source is conspiring to send a step in your direction that you must take first. Be open to the information you receive around you, for nothing is random.

Make sure that your thoughts are positive surrounding the reality that you want to attract. If you have bad feelings or negativity surrounding you, then you, in reality, are conspiring against yourself.

Be sure of what you want to attract into your life because only if your focus is directed with conviction and positive energy, can you begin to magnetize it. Can you imagine going shopping, but not being sure about what you want to buy? If you are not sure about what you want to buy, then you may end up buying nothing or buying something you do not even want. Such is the law of attraction. You cannot magnetize any reality that you desire if your focus is unclear.

Magnetizing your desires is an easy thing if you know what to do.

The first thing is to be clear about what you want. Being clear about what you want helps you to project a clear visualization of your desired reality.

The second thing you must do is be firmly rooted in your belief around the desired reality. If you are clear about what you want, but do not think you can acquire it, then you will not attract it because your overpowering belief is the lack of what you desire; therefore, you will attract the lack that you truly believe in. Instead, focus with clarity on what you want and focus on a true heart felt belief that it will come into being.

The third thing you must do is be aware of the situations that the Source sends to you, for these situations might be, or usually are, indeed, stepping stones that lead to your desired reality. Be open to the opportunities that come your way, no matter how small you think they are. A small opportunity could very well be the first step to the reality you are desiring to attract. Do not shut yourself to the assistance that the Source is sending, but be open to receiving. Remember also, that you must activate yourself. If you want to magnetize an event, it is not good to sit in your armchair and wait for it to knock on your door. You must be willing to activate yourself and to take the required steps to seize that which the Source is sending to you. Remember that when you focus on something, the Universe conspires to magnetize it for you, but you must also seize the moment and take the required steps in its direction.

So having the thought and the belief may not necessarily be enough to materialize your desires. You're saying that it is important to take action as well.

Yes. Being an armchair participant is not a good option or way to live your life. You must be in partnership with the Source. If what you attract shows up on your doorstep and you do not answer the door, it will turn around and walk away, so it is important to recognize the opportunities that the Source sends you and to embrace them with the action that you must take. Make it a habit to be open to what the Source sends to you when magnetism is at play, for if magnetism is to work for you, then you must embrace it when it knocks on your door.

Meditation is the key to convincing your brain that it can happen. Your brain, or rather, your ego, tends to get in the way at times, and this is why there are times when manifestation is harder than it should be.

Meditate on that which you want to attract, and hold the visualization of the event or thing in your mind. Always hold the belief that it is already yours, and it will help the Universe in materializing it for you. Keep the visual clear and keep your focus clear, and it will take root within your subconscious mind. If you hold any doubts, then these doubts will become the overpowering belief that will thwart the materialization of your desire. Hold the visual of what you desire with clarity. Become convinced in its materialization, and make the belief strong in your mind. Once you are clear, then the Universe will be clear, and the Source can help to bring it into your reality. By being clear, you are telling yourself that you can truly acquire that which you desire.

Visualize all that is connected to your desire. If you desire a car, then visualize the color and model of the car. Visualize every detail of the car; the tires, the year, and make of the vehicle. Put yourself in the driver's seat and visualize yourself driving the car. Sense the smells and the scenery as you drive it. Make it real within your mind and believe that you are there. The brain cannot distinguish between imagination and reality. It will react to both in the same manner. By doing this exercise, you will put yourself in the frame of mind that your brain would be in if this reality truly existed, and it would proceed in a direction that partners with the Source in the materialization of the car and events leading up to the ownership of your vehicle. Do this with all things that you would desire, and your reality will take a new direction.

Melanie: Make sure that your desires are loving and good, for this is the true path of the Source's quest. Desiring bad or evil events can only lead to negative situations and ill will for all concerned. Let love be your guide and let love lead you towards your goals in life. Love of self is noble, and there is nothing wrong with desiring things for oneself. It is good to desire wealth and good possessions, although some think that it is selfish. Believe us when we tell you that the quest of the Source is as selfish as it is altruistic, and all experience is valuable.

Yes, many people do believe that it is selfish and wrong to desire or have wealth. What would you say to these people to help them move beyond this and realize that it is fine to have wealth? This is something that I still struggle with as well.

Wealth is but an avenue of experience that a Source soul utilizes for the purpose of learning lessons. It is not evil, and it is not good. It is neutral. If money is termed evil in a situation, then it is important to look at the person who is utilizing this money in such a fashion because it is this person who needs to be aware of his efforts surrounding money. If money is deemed to be good, then again, it is the person utilizing this money who is doing good. Money is something that man has always struggled with, and it is a part of your learning journey. There is nothing wrong with money and having it. It is only wrong when having money leads to wrongful deeds against a human or the planet.

Money is polluting your planet at this time because some corporations pay no heed to the results of their conquest and greed. Meditate on all things that you struggle with, and therein lay your answers.

Your quest is also the Source's quest, and your desires are the Source's desires. There is no separation between you and the Source other than the illusion of separation, and we would urge you to follow and attain your dreams and desires in the quest for self-actualization.

Part of the problem you have today is that many of you do not believe that you are worthy to receive that which you desire, and many of you have guilt associated with desiring good things for yourself. Many of these beliefs are ingrained through your lives by many of the people who influence you. Religion has also been a contributing factor in this guilt and lack of deserving in your lives. Remember that every father wants the best for his children, and the Source is no different than a loving parent, and it is truly all in your head. When you begin to realize this, then magnetism will work more easily for you, and the situations you desire will manifest themselves more easily.

Be present in your body, mind, and soul, and be always aware of the energy you create. Does your energy attract or repel? Being present will help you to manipulate your magnetism and will help to create and attract the reality that you want. You are more in control than you realize, and magnetism is easier to manipulate than you realize. The entire Universe of your reality is governed by magnetism or the law of attraction, as you term it. Be aware of your energy and be conscious of how you use it, as well as whether it is positive or negative. Remember that positive attracts and negative repels. If you want something, but have negative energy, you will repel it, and what you end up attracting may not be the best situation for you. Use your magnetism wisely, for it is very real indeed, and it will either attract or repel situations in your life. Meditate and be present within yourself, and you will see results.

Many of you feel that magnetism is not a real and justified thing, but if you would put your doubts aside for a moment and try it, you would begin to notice subtle changes in your reality and in your lives. We must urge you to try it and see for yourselves. Give it a chance and you will be astounded at the results. Be patient with yourself and in time it will pay off, and the difference in your life will be astounding. Make it a conscious decision to live your life in the light of the Source, for this is the light that powers magnetism and gives you the reality that you desire.

We spoke of being clear of what you desire and of visualizing it as an existing reality. Make it clear and real within your mind, and soon you will notice that events and situations will begin to transpire. Be aware of these events, for the Source will begin to fulfill your desire by sending these events your way. Be open to receiving that which the Source sends to you because it is not always the obvious path that will be sent to you, and therefore, you must be open to receive and interpret the signals that are sent.

Em: Be patient, for these events take time in your reality, and they will appear when the time is right for you. Always be open to receive that which the Source is sending you, and be prepared to seize the opportunity no matter how big or small it appears to be. If you maintain this openness to receive, you will be able to utilize the law of attraction to your benefit. It is not enough to be clear and to visualize that which you would like to manifest. You must be willing to take the steps necessary and seize the opportunities that come your way. In this manner, your desired destiny will manifest itself. If you desire or visualize that which you want, but do not seize the moment as it is presented to you, then you will send conflicting messages to the Source, and your magnetism will begin to repel that which you desire. Be positive to the possibilities that are presented to you no matter how small they may appear. Do not dismiss their significance, for even a small event that may seem insignificant may be the event that leads to your desire, ultimately. Nothing is random and nothing is insignificant.

All roads lead to your desired event, and all roads must be taken seriously if you want to materialize that which you desire.

Faking your emotions around the visualization of that which you desire, will not attract it to you. You must be sincere in your belief and your emotions surrounding the event or thing that you desire. Be sincere and be truthful to yourself, for this is very important in making magnetism work for you. Remember that everything is powered by magnetic energy, and this includes your beliefs, thoughts, and emotions. Your actions are also powered by magnetic energy, and nothing is exempt from it, not even the tiniest speck in the Universe. All is energy, all is light, all emanates from the Source, and it is yours as well, and you are a part of the Source, and you and we are of Source.

Be open to receiving that which the Universe is sending you at all times, and follow the inner voice that guides you, for it is the voice of the Source who dwells within your heart and soul. Be in God's light and be true to your purpose in your lifetime and current reality. Love one another and love yourself as you would love another. We say that because some of you love others more than you love yourself, and it is all relative. You are love incarnated and sometimes, or we should say most times, you forget that. Remember that love has magnetic energy that attracts, and you should surround that which you want to manifest with the energy of love. We must impress this upon you, for many of you dwell not on what you love, but on what you hate, and this is why you experience negative situations in your lives.

Be conscious of your thoughts, for they possess energy, and magnetic energy does not distinguish between right and wrong or good and evil. It is simply energy, and it magnetizes what you dwell on. Replace your negative thoughts with good thoughts when you find yourself spiraling into negativity, and remember that magnetism is everywhere and permeates everything, whether it is a solid mass or a thought. You are in control, whether you believe it or not. You create your own reality through your thoughts and belief systems. Be aware of this.

We spoke of belief systems in an earlier chapter. We spoke of how to change these belief systems to better serve yourselves, and part of this equation is the law of attraction or magnetism, as we call it. Magnetism is the tool that you have at your disposal to shape your reality, and many of you do not take full advantage in utilizing this tool. Be aware of it, and use it to shape a better life for yourself. It is the substance that permeates the entire Universe, both seen and unseen, and it is a very powerful tool. It is always at your disposal, and it is shaping your life whether you are conscious of it or not, so the best approach is to live your life consciously and be aware of the unseen as well as the seen Universe.

Be aware that if we reduced the realities that exist into their smallest components, all that would exist is light and the energy of light. All That Is, is light and energy coupled with conscious awareness, and it is through this conscious awareness that all of the realities and sub-worlds emanate from. You are all a part of this conscious energy, and it is through cooperation with the Source that all realities exist, and it is through this energy that your reality exists; both your Universe, planet, and personal reality. Be a conscious part of this reality when shaping your own world, and use the energy of the Source to create your world through magnetism and the law of attraction. Meditate, and create your reality and all that you desire.

Melanie: This chapter is to be called.......

Chapter Twelve:

Alternate Realities

Melanie: Your current reality is but a small section of the realities that exist, and you are currently dwelling in other realities as well as this one. How can this be so, you ask? Quite simply, if you can grasp the concept that all time happens at once. In other words, time is only linear in your dimension of experience, or, should we say, in a few dimensions of experience, but if you remove the linear concept of time, then all reality exists in the now, and your soul has many components that exist simultaneously in the now.

What do you mean when you say that our soul has many components?

Your soul has many components that are a part of your oversoul. Each compartment or part of your oversoul is experiencing a section of reality on behalf of the oversoul. Liken it to a body which is comprised of many parts that allow it to operate. Each portion of your soul makes up your

153

soul in its entirety, just as each body part makes up your body in its entirety.

Can you explain to us what an oversoul is?

An oversoul is the Source soul unit that the Source sent forth to experience the many planes and realities in an effort for self-actualization. Each Source soul sent out portions of itself for the same purpose. This is why you can experience many reincarnations in the non-linear now. The non-linear now, meaning not controlled by linear time. Make it a habit to open your mind in an effort to understand the concepts that we are explaining to you, for we understand that these concepts do not fall within the reasoning of the human mind.

Are you saying that all of our reincarnational lives are being lived at the same time? How can this be?

It is in the now, but not as you understand it to be. The now is hard to comprehend by the three dimensional human mind. It is a concept that operates well in our dimension, and it does not mean that you are concurrently living millions of lives. You experience each life separately, but all lives occur in the now of our dimension. Think of each moment that you inhabit as the now, and then you may realize that each now is moment to moment, but your personality only experiences each moment as it happens. It is really quite a simple concept if you do not try to over analyze it. It is easier than mankind imagines.

Time is linear in your dimension, and therefore, there must be a beginning and an ending. In our dimension, there is no structured time as you understand it, and we can travel at will in what you would term forward or backward in time. This is due to the abstraction of time. It is an abstract to you when it does not follow a structured course. Because time is an abstract, it does not really exist except for in your dimension, and this is for the reason of keeping you focused and anchored as you dwell in your reality. You could easily spend many years trying to wrap your three dimensional mind around a non dimensional concept. Time exists solely for your benefit.

If we are inhabiting many realities concurrently, why is it that we are only experiencing and aware of this one reality?

Because your mind, that is rooted in this dimension, must focus itself in this dimension, otherwise it would bleed over into other realities and other realities would bleed through to this one. It would cause you to become unfocused, and it would be as if you had many personalities within one. It would cause chaos and confusion in the plane you inhabit.

Is there any other part of us that is focused in these other realities?

Yes. It is, at times, your dream state that focuses on other realities. This may come to you in the form of a dream in which you may see yourself as another person in that dream. Many dreams that you have are visits to these other reincarnations. These dream states offer you the opportunity to visit other realities such as those you have lived in your past lives. They may come as glimpses of your activities just before death in a particular life. If you have a fear of water in this lifetime, you may dream of a time when you were in water just before drowning in a previous lifetime. These glimpses are soul memories experienced as dreams. You may also visit places of learning during your dream states, and these dreams offer an opportunity for growth while you sleep. You may or may not remember these dreams upon wakening. These are a few examples of that which we speak.

If time exists as the "now" outside of our Earthly linear time, then when we reincarnate, do we necessarily reincarnate into a future time or can we reincarnate into a past time?

Yes, there is no order of linear time that you must follow when you reincarnate. It is possible, when you leave this lifetime, to reincarnate into what you would term as the past. In our level it is the now, which is occurring concurrently in your understanding. What we experience as the now has no definition such as mankind's experience of linear time. We experience moment to moment as we so choose. We can travel into your past or future, but to us it is simply another moment of now. If you were to translate this experience into your definition of linear time, you would perceive all as occurring concurrently, although in your dimension, it would translate itself into a linear timeline.

So in your reality, cause and effect all happen at the same time.

Yes. It is instant. As we think, we experience instantly as we are transported to the event or the event rushes towards us. In your dimension, a passing of time must occur.

Think of reincarnation, and you may understand how you can inhabit many lifetimes of reality, and then think of time as the now, and you will begin to see how you can inhabit many realities concurrently. Reincarnation is a very real concept, and we will discuss this now.

You would be limited in your thinking to believe that you inhabit only one lifetime and then die and go to the other side for eternity. You are a part of the Source that is seeking to understand itself through self-actualization, and therefore, this life you currently lead is a part of that quest.

You have come to this Earth plane in your specific body, in this specific time, to learn a specific lesson, and have a specific experience. This is but one lifetime of experience, and when your time on this planet is over, you may decide to re-enter it again to learn additional lessons and have additional experiences. Make no mistake in understanding this. You have been here before, and you will come here again. We have also had lifetimes on Earth, and we will be back for additional lifetimes. At this time, as you know time, we have decided to stay here while you have decided to inhabit Earth.

Many of your lifetimes are spent with familiar souls, and you have all experienced these lifetimes in different capacities of relationships with each other. Sometimes you have been sisters, and sometimes you have been lovers, while other times you have been enemies. This is all in the quest for different experiences with each other, and in order to gain these experiences, your roles have been interchangeable.

Em: All of these experiences and lifetimes are for the purpose of the Source's experience towards self-actualization, and this has led to the expansion of each individual Source soul's self-actualization as well. It has also led to the expansion of your Universe, for as the Source's realization expands, it causes your Universe to expand, and this is why you perceive your Universe as expanding as opposed to shrinking. Your Universe will never shrink.

Many scientists believe that the Universe will eventually implode and some philosophies say that the Universe will go through a resting phase. You say our Universe will never shrink. What will really happen in the Universe's evolution? Will it ever implode or rest?

No. All of the Universe is expanding due to the nature of the Source's journey of self-actualization and self expression. There are realities being birthed as we speak, and this contributes to the expansion of the Universe. It is a level of expansion that is growing with every thought that is experienced within the Source, for as the Source thinks, the Source becomes, and the Source is a powerhouse of thought and energy, as you would term it. As the Universe expands through Source thought, new realities and new matter is continually birthed, and these take on form in an evolutionary sense in your terms. The Universe is full of movement and expansion. There is no stagnation in the Universe, for such stagnation would cause shrinkage as old worlds die and nothing would materialize to replace them.

As old worlds die?

Think of the lifespan of a star and its surrounding planets. If a star such as your sun were to die, this would surely cause your world's death as well.

Then in order for the Universe to continue expanding, new realities and worlds would have to be birthed at a faster pace than old worlds are dying at.

Yes. You also have other levels of realities that exist concurrently with yours. These too, are expanding and probabilities are also multiplying.

And it is all growing exponentially.

Yes.

Here's what I have a hard time following. If everything exists in the now, then this would include every probable reality and every new emerging reality, in which case everything that could possibly be experienced by the Source, already exists. So how is it continuing to expand?

We understand your confusion, for it is expressed by many on your planet, but the now is expanding also, and it will never cease because although time does not exist, it does not mean that all is static in a state of final expectation. It is an energetic Universe of now, and we like to experience many things, even on our level, and this causes us to create new things that become instantaneously visible in the now. We understand that this is a difficult concept for you, and this is why we have asked you to read this book with an open mind to all possibilities. Think of it as everything existing in the now, even possibilities that have yet to occur. The now encompasses all that currently exists and all possibilities waiting to exist.

Be aware of the relationships in your life, and try to learn the lessons that you can glean from the experiences you share with one another, and your purpose for being here will not be lost on you.

When you decided to enter this Earth plane, you made many choices that were to govern and accompany your experiences here on Earth. You chose your gender, your parents who were to accompany you on this journey, and you chose your friends and relatives, and so forth. You chose the country of your birth and the era of your experience. Be assured once more that nothing about your reality is random, and that everything is with purpose in your lifetime here and in all of your lifetimes on planet Earth.

You have chosen this life and all the elements surrounding your life, but be assured that all of your experience was not set in stone. This is where free will enters the picture, and all of these experiences unfold as you set your belief system and set the course of your decisions. As a result of these decisions and beliefs, your life experiences unfold as an improvisational play on the stage of your reality. You can change or alter the outcome at any time by simply altering your beliefs or changing the course of your destiny through the decisions you make. If you were to go to a psychic, your reading could be correct and unfold as foretold, but at any time, this course can be changed by altering your course through free will, so this is why not all psychic readings are correct, frauds aside.

Make sure you lead your life with true and loving purpose, and be true to yourself, and let not others lead you from your path. At the same time, you must allow others to live their own lives and without the need to have ownership over others. Live and let live in the loving light of the Source. Be mindful and respectful towards others, for they have their own purpose for being here, and it is not for us to dictate the terms of their journey and experiences here on this plane called Earth. You would have fuller journeys of understanding if you would allow others their space. Your lives would be smoother if you would realize this.

Melanie: Your current reality is one that exists, of many. Reincarnated lives are other levels of reality. In your terms, when you die, you leave this reality and go back from whence you came. Your time on Earth is measured in your time units, and it progresses in a linear fashion. When you are between lives, there is no unit of time measurement, and all exists in the now. Your decisions, here on Earth, have outcomes and certain results, but the result will lead in a specific direction. If you changed the course by reacting to any specific situation differently, it would have a different outcome. This is where we lead this topic to the area of probable realities and probable selves.

Imagine, if you will, a grid system, and this grid system had intersecting lines. Consider these intersecting lines as separate points of three dimensional reality, and each point of intersection would represent the probable outcome of any specific course you might have taken in your life. Each course is a reflection of you in various realities and various probable outcomes, and these exist all at once. Let us give you an example of this.

A man is walking down the street. He comes to a crosswalk. He decides to cross without looking and is struck by a vehicle. This reality now unfolds with regards to the ongoing result of this decision. A probable decision may have been to stop and look, and he crosses without incident and makes it safely across. This probable reality now plays itself out to its final outcome. These probable realities exist at once and will play themselves out in this lifetime, but at different points on the grid of reality. Imagine that these realities are playing themselves out for every one on this planet, and imagine the different results and courses that are playing out simultaneously. This is what your probable realities would look like; and they co-exist for us all. In one reality, you might be a Doctor, and in another reality, your decisions and beliefs may have led you to be a Vet, and these probable realities are playing themselves out concurrently in life. Why would they exist, you ask? The answer is simple. The Source is experiencing all aspects of your life, including all of the probable outcomes, and this is simply for the experience of the Source's quest for self-actualization.

Can you explain this a little further? I'm trying to understand where these probable realities exist.

Yes. We are talking about the different planes that are occupied by these probable realities. We use the grid as a visual type tool to explain the concept. Each probable reality occupies another level or plane of reality, just as your reality occupies the plane of your reality. The plane, being the current three dimensional reality that you reside in.

This brings me back to a question I had about reincarnation and the concept that we dwell in more than one reality concurrently. Is it also possible to reincarnate back into lives we have already experienced? Can I repeat my current life if I so desired, and would there be any reason to do so?

No, it would be redundant.

Would it be possible to do so if we so choose?

You have no reason to because each life serves the exact purpose it was intended for. It would be like having a loop that replays exactly the same thing over and over again. This is what your probable scenarios are for.

How do all of our probable scenarios fit in, then? Is there any part of us that is experiencing those?

Yes. The oversoul experiences it as a whole, just as the Source experiences us all as a whole. Think of oversouls as microcosms of the Source.

In which case, it is each of the components of the oversouls that is experiencing all of the probable realities.

Yes. It is simple.

So, just to confirm; you are saying that all probable realities exist on some level and get played out whether or not we personally experience them within this lifetime?

Yes. The oversoul, and the Source benefits from these probabilities.

Em: What determines the outcome of your current probable reality, you may ask? You do. Your set of beliefs surrounding your life and your set of decisions as a result of the beliefs you hold surrounding any given situation. In a previous chapter, we told you that if you want to change your life, then you must change your mind. This applies at all times and circumstances in your life. It is easier than you think, and you can change your life at any time and set it on a different probable course. This ties in very well with the chapter on belief systems, and you are truly in charge of your life and all of its probable outcomes.

Melanie: You are capable of charting any probability of your reality, and it is easier than you think. Your doubts and fears have an effect on the outcome in any given case, and if you would operate on a level without fears and doubts, then your desired outcome in any given situation would flow more easily and take the direction you desire. Simply chart your reality, and take the steps you chart and become a partner with the Source, and allow magnetism to take the lead as you follow with the corresponding steps.

What do you mean when you tell us to simply chart our reality?

Many of you refer to this as setting goals. We mean that you should plan what you want in life just as a teenager attending high school should plan and decide what he wants to do with his life. Your plan and life chart is a chart of your goals and desires.

Your probable selves and their probable outcomes already exist, and one of them will become your specific reality. In the reality you desire, your probable self already exists, and you can access this probable self through magnetism. Be in contact with the future that you desire, and draw it to you. Magnetism is your partner. The probable self that already exists, can reach back and draw you near. Imagine this probable self as reaching back in time and giving you the answers you need at this time to draw you into the probable reality that you desire to manifest. Be at one with this future self and it will draw itself to you in this reality. Be not afraid and have no doubts, for these doubts will alter the outcome.

I love this concept of reaching out to your future probable self. Can we communicate with our future probable selves? Can we ask them to help guide us to them? How can we access our successful future probable selves and make this concept work for us?

Through meditation and visualization. Imagine yourself as you would want to be in your future. If you want to own your own successful business, then visualize this as being a current reality, and visualize all that this success would encompass. See yourself in this picture surrounded by all that your success would contain. Visualize yourself asking your future self to step back and give you the advice and help that will get you to where you desire. This is a game you can play that is a useful tool in manifesting that which you desire.

(During the break here, Tina and I began a discussion where we compared life to a large playground. This whole

concept reminded us of being at play, where we could choose to experience any reality we wanted. There is no end to the probabilities we can choose from. We just have to focus on what we truly desire, and this focus will begin to manifest it for us. This led to the following commentary.)

Melanie: Your analogy of the playground is correct, and we will incorporate this now. Imagine that all of life is a playground and that you are the children that are playing. You can choose the game that you want to play, and you can choose the rules and outcome of this game. You are the conductor and orchestrater, and you can play the game to your desired outcome. Do so with the game you call your life. Meditation is the key, and we must express this with conviction. Make it a habit to meditate every day, and your desired realities will flow more easily.

You are on a planet that experiences three dimensional reality and is governed by space, time, and volume. It exists in a Universe that is inhabited by other galaxies, stars, planets, and so forth. At no time are you alone in this Universe, for there are other realities that exist on other planets. Some of these realities exist microscopically, and others exist on a larger level. Some of these realities have intersected with yours and they question your reality just as you question theirs. Make no mistake about it; they do exist, and they have visited your planet, and they have interacted with many of you.

You have not to fear, for they will not destroy you. It is not their purpose. All of their efforts have been in an attempt to understand your species and its destructive nature. They view you as a threat at this time because of your destructive nature, and they want to keep an eye on you, per se.

You say that we have not to fear these other realities, but how can we be certain of this? Are there realities of a lower or negative frequency that exist? And if so, how do we know that they would not try to harm us?

Meditate on good, and you will attract good. Meditate on evil, and you will create evil. It is a part of magnetism which is your law of attraction.

But what about in reference to other life forms that are visiting us?

We would advise you to be a peaceful world, for it is through love and peace that you can live in brotherhood with those who visit you. It is at this time in your reality that you are being visited by what you term as aliens. These aliens are peaceful, and they are watching over you so that you do not literally blow yourselves up, for this would affect their worlds as well, through the imbalance that you would create in the Universe, for it would be far reaching. They are also quite amazed and impressed with your life form, and would want to protect its existence. They are like the parent who is protecting a child from harming himself. They are far more advanced and knowledgeable than you, such as a parent is to his small child. The child is young and naïve, and requires protection from the parent. These visitors are much more advanced and regard you as such a child.

The Earth experience is unique in that it encompasses love, birth, growth, and transformation on many levels, from human, to plant, to animal, to cellular. It is a Garden of Eden that is wondrous to behold. It is likened to a flower garden of brilliance in the center of a bleak landscape. Your species is an experiment of love, thought, growth, procreation, and most of all, grand evolution from elementary beginnings. The beauty of your planet is rather astounding for your visitors to behold, and they regard it as a jewel of great brilliance. It is a shame that all of this is elusive to mankind, and his blindness promotes the destruction of such beauty.

Make it a habit to meditate, and you will come to know who they are. They communicate with their minds as they are more advanced than you, and their thoughts can traverse space and time just as yours can. You are simply not aware of this concept yet, and therefore, you do not know how to utilize it. They are available to those who would seek peaceful and loving purpose. Meditate to connect, and you will connect with them. (To Tina and Tilde: You are at a place where this is possible, for your minds are open and ready.) For those readers of this material; those of you who are open and ready are also capable to do so. Yes this is true, for we are ready to help you bridge realities.

Have faith that the time will come when much more will be revealed to you all, but not until your spiritual growth has made you prepared to receive that which would frighten you at this phase of your intellectual development. Make it a practice to live a spiritual life and live your life in the Source's light. Laugh and be content in God's light.

You say that not everything will be revealed to us at this time because it could frighten us. Why would we be frightened if you revealed much more to us?

Because you are not advanced enough yet to understand or see the whole picture, as you would term it. An example of this is the alien experience. If these people from the other worlds were to suddenly and openly reveal themselves, there would be much fear on your part. There would also be much death on your part, literally, from heart attacks that would occur.

The visitors who have come to this planet are from another galaxy of life, and they experience reality much differently than you do. They are intellectual beings, and their reality is based on intellect that is far more advanced than yours. Their intellect is how they, as a mass of spiritual beings, decided to experience the Source's self-actualization, and their rules of engagement were predetermined before they came to inhabit their bodies and their reality.

This is but one example of another reality, although many more exist. We have chosen to discuss this particular one because these beings are the ones who have contacted your civilization. They have developed advanced systems of travel that you will not be able to emulate for many centuries to come, for that is how advanced they are. *They* first became aware of *you*, for they, just as yourselves, were interested in exploring the possibilities of life on other planets. They have discovered you a long time ago, and it was in the early phase of mankind. They have studied your development and charted your progress without interference, for this would have been inappropriate according to their rules of engagement. Yes, they have abducted you, and yes they have studied you, but none of this has been for evil purposes. It has been in an effort to understand you and chart your evolution. They would not dare make contact with a race of warriors, for their purpose would be peaceful, and they would wait until your evolution has progressed to such a level. You are not ready for contact with these beings, and by you, we are referring to the human race as a whole. There are those of you on Earth who are spiritually and peacefully ready, and there has been contact with some of you. We would urge the human race to become peaceful and united.

You mentioned that alien races have visited us and have charted our progress. Have they had anything to do with the evolution of mankind, and if so, what?

Yes, many races from other planets have visited Earth from many eons ago until this day and beyond. They became fascinated with your planet and species a very long time ago, and as they do now, they abducted human specimens at that time as well. They have produced hybrids that you have not seen because they are in the process of creating a new species that is a blend of you and them. They have done this in the past with mankind, and you are the result. A much improved race of mankind.

This sounds more like science fiction than reality. I'm not sure how people will respond to this.

Think of your scientists who are currently producing hybrids of plant life and animal life, and then apply it to alien life. Think of these aliens as scientists who are doing the same as mankind's scientists. Instead of producing hybrid plant life, they have experimented with intelligent life.

But isn't this against our will? I'm sure people would feel extremely violated by this.

Yes, and many have felt violated, but mankind is the result of such experimentation and you are quite content with the outcome today.

I don't know what to think. I don't know what people reading this will think.

We understand that it is outrageous in your reasoning, but there are those of you who are already embracing this concept.

You have evolved from a much more primitive source. Left on its own, this primitive source would not have evolved to its current state without the intervention and cross breeding with a higher intelligent being. There is much written today on this subject, and mankind is beginning to psychically become aware of his beginnings. Part of your awakening is time encapsulated within your genetic code. This is to be further discussed in your next book.

Your contact with these beings has been sporadic, but consistent throughout your evolution. At first, they discovered you as a result of searching for other realities, but as your civilization progressed, they continued to contact you as a result of signals sent by you. Such signals as radio frequencies and so forth. Make no mistake about it; other civilizations do exist, and connections will be made when the time is right for your world.

How can they travel, you ask? They are far more advanced than you, and they understand the law of magnetism and have harnessed its power. Magnetism can propel at great speeds, but still not fast enough to cross galaxies. There are points of intersection where time and reality intersect. These points of intersection are utilized as jump points or entry points. By manipulating these points of intersection, they have been able to traverse great distances by not physically having to travel the entirety of that distance. So you see, this is but an example of another reality. When the time is right, contact will be made, but as we said, not for many centuries to come, for your race is still an aggressive race, full of fear and hatred towards some elements that it does not understand. Contact is being currently made, but mankind is not ready for full assimilation into the Universal community, for there are alien races who are aware of, and in contact with each other. This will be further explored in your next book. Make a part of your purpose the quest for peace and love.

Can you tell us a little more about how these beings travel? I'd like to know more about the vehicles they use and of these jump points that you mentioned.

They travel in ships, as you have observed. Some of these ships are for the purpose of shorter quests, and some are for the purpose of longer quests. The large ships that you term mother ships are for the longer journeys that involve what you would term time travel. That is, traveling great distances in seconds. The smaller ships dwell within the mother ship, and these are used for the smaller excursions they undertake when they have arrived on your planet. They also have smaller units of observation that are unmanned for the purpose of reconnaissance. These can be as small as one of your cameras or smaller. You would term them as probes.

Jump points are points in the Universal world where planes intersect. In this intersection, they have located what could be termed as a door or a crossover where they intersect with one another. It is like opening a door at this intersection and walking into another room; the room being your dimension. This is how they do it, and this is how you will do it when you have developed to that level, but not until after your third eye is open and you have become a fully peaceful race.

Why have there been so many U.F.O. sightings recently? It seems that they would really like to make their presence known.

They are concerned about the state of your planet and would like to help if they could, but it is not appropriate to interfere with the affairs of mankind. They are making their own attempts, such as we are, to give information to spiritual beings that inhabit Earth, in an attempt to avert that which mankind might do unto himself and this planet.

But they would step in if we were to destroy ourselves?

Yes, but not until such a time would occur, if at all because of free will. It would affect other dimensions as well, and they occupy these dimensions. In other words, your self annihilation would cause them much harm. Everything is connected. Think of it as a pebble thrown into a body of water. It has a ripple effect.

But our self annihilation still exists as a probability?

All probabilities exist and this includes their dimensions as well. It would, therefore, exist as a probability for them also.

Em: Your galaxy has many planets with life forms, and you are but an example of one of these life forms. Make no mistake; they do exist. Your form is but one example of this, and your reality is determined by the atmosphere and elements of the planet you dwell on. Other forms of life are governed by the elements that shape their reality and environment. This is just one example, and when your time is right, you will begin to explore other planets just as your visitors have explored you.

The reality that your visitors live in is much different than yours. They have learned how to manipulate realities because they understand the power of the mind and the illusion of time and matter. In gaining an understanding of these elements, they have learned to manipulate your reality as they travel within it. This is why they can remain undetected in your world. In doing so, they can observe you with little or no detection, and therefore, you remain mostly unaware of their visits. They have the ability to suspend the electromagnetic energy that allows detection. They do not eliminate this energy. They simply neutralize it while they visit you. After their visit, you may wake up and get a sense that someone has been there, but at the same time, it does not seem to make sense to you. You may notice a disruption in your electrical power, and you may notice a silence and deadness of atmosphere. You may also notice vain attempts to arouse others from their deep slumber. You have been visited if this is what you awaken to.

You mentioned that they have the ability to suspend or neutralize electromagnetic energy. What does this mean, and how does it work?

Melanie: It is at times of visitations that they are able to neutralize your energy, and we mean exactly that. You will notice that you have not the ability to move. It is as if you have been put into a deep freeze. They eliminate your electricity where they are approaching, and because they put everything concerned into a state of suspended animation, they are able to come and go without notice or incident during an abduction. This is why many of you become paralyzed. This is why the electricity is suspended, and this is why you have trouble waking up others in your household when such an event has occurred. The members of your household are put into a deep sleep so they will not awaken and notice that you are gone.

You are but one of many that have been visited.

Are you referring to the general reader here, or are you referring to Tilde and me?

Em: You and Tilde. You have been visited since childhood, and the reason is because your sensitivity has alerted them. There are those of you that have been visited as well for this very reason.

There are some people who will be in total disbelief of this, and there will be others who will find this all to be quite disturbing.

We would advise you to read this book with an open mind. There are some who will simply not be ready to accept this information because they are not in a level of their journey where they have advanced to a place where this information is easily digested. In other words, portions of mankind are not evolved to the level that others have evolved to. This is just a fact and result of separate journeys. We would not worry because bit by bit, your third eye will open, and it too is a journey.

This is to lead us into our next chapter to be titled.......

Chapter Thirteen:

The Awakening

Melanie: Many of you here on Earth are sensitive beings who are beginning to have experiences in reality that you are questioning, and many of you are sensitive in a nature that we will refer to as a psychic sense of being. You have been born on Earth during a time of great upheaval and yet great progress, and there are those who are leading civilization on a quest of self awareness and an opening of mankind's third eye. You have all chosen to come here at this great time in the development of your planet, and yours is a journey of self discovery and revelation for the rest of mankind. We are here to assist you in this quest, and we have made much progress, but there is still a greater road to travel ahead. You were not put here at this time by accident, and you chose to be a part of this great heralding time.

You say that this is a time of great upheaval and yet great progress. What is this upheaval that you speak of?

There are those of you who are not developed as others, and as a result, are still stuck in old systems of belief patterns. These would include civilizations among you who are oppressing their populations as well as those among you who are engaged in wars with each other. There is also great planetary upheaval, and this is witnessed in the many hurricanes, tornados, earthquakes, and other shifting weather and geological shifts on your planet. At the same time, there are many among you who are choosing a spiritual path of growth and understanding. These two elements are opposing elements at this time, and it will eventually give way to the growth that is to come.

So are you saying that the awakening of mankind will prevail?

Yes. Absolutely because it is a part of mankind's quest.

Then, does that not mean that destruction of this planet and destruction of mankind would not take place?

No. It means that mankind's determination will prevail, but due to free will, mankind can always change the balance. You must understand that at this time there is great destruction and opposing forces on your planet, and it may take a destructive event to shock mankind to his senses.

We certainly hope it doesn't come to that.

It can be avoided through mankind's shift in awareness and his action for change.

Why are some of us experiencing this psychic awakening, and not others?

Mankind is about to undertake the first steps towards the awakening of his third eye. Many of you are on different paths on different sections of this journey, and this means that there are some of you who are further along the path of development. Some souls will develop their awakening in future lives, while others of you are leading the way with the beginnings of your awakening in this current lifetime.

Demna: You have always been aware of the differences between you and others that are not so sensitive. We want to clarify that when we speak of you, we are addressing those readers who have this awareness; and there are many. All of your lives you have experienced a different kind of reality than those who you have in your circle of friends and family. Your experiences throughout life have made you aware that there is another reality that you can access, and this has at times troubled you and frightened you, for you have had no reference points with which to compare these experiences. You have sought medical treatment, you have sought psychiatric treatment, and you have sought information from many books and sources that deal with the phenomenon of the unknown. Be aware that you are normal, and that no illness is afflicting you. You are sane in an insane world.

Many of you will know what we talk of, as you read this chapter, and we are trying to open these channels in you further, for it is time to awaken the sleeper within you. Your experiences have been similar, and at times you have questioned them and wondered why this is happening, and why it is happening to you and not others. You have had experiences that many classify as paranormal; outside the normal of the frame of reference of your plane of existence. We will talk about these experiences.

Many of you had invisible friends as children, or you saw entities that are not considered of this world. These friends have been your guides and friends through life, and though you may not see us now, you did see us at a time in your lives. Our purpose has been to keep you safe and guide you through your lives, and we will continue to guide you through your awakening. We will always be with you.

Many of you have experienced out of body episodes, and these episodes are for a reason. Because you are sensitives, you have been able to disengage from your physical bodies from time to time. The purpose for this exercise is to make you aware of the other reality by disengaging from this one. In this way, you can keep your awareness open.

Em: Your experiences have been for many purposes. They have been intended to make you aware of the existence of this other reality. They have been for the purpose of making you aware of your divinity, and they have been utilized as a method to jolt you into awareness. They are to remind you of the purpose you chose when you entered this reality. Some of these experiences have frightened you. We urge you not to fear, for there is nothing to be afraid of. Be aware, for that is the intent.

Many of you, at times, have experienced precognition. This is also part of your awakening. There are many shared experiences. We spoke of visitations, and these have been experienced by many of you sensitives. You have been visited because your energy patterns are different than those of you who are asleep. Those of you who have been visited have drawn this attention because your energy vibration is different than those who are asleep. Your vibrational energy is higher than others, but still low enough so that you inhabit dense form. When your vibration increased, you attracted attention and the visitors came to you. They are aware of your heightened sensitivity and chose to examine and study you. Many of you have been quite awake and aware of these visits, though you retain no conscious memory of them. This is to protect you from fallout that would be experienced in your reality and to keep your civilization from arming itself against a society that is peaceful and advanced. It is for your protection and theirs. If you retained your memories, some of you would remember that you have formed friendships with these individuals, and they have visited you often, not only to study you, but to prepare your civilization for its awakening. You have had many experiences that are outside the realm of normal as your society knows it, and deep inside you all know who you are.

When you compare sensitives to those who are asleep, what do you mean by asleep?

176

Melanie: We mean those portions of mankind who are not yet spiritually aware.

You say that our visitors are here, not only to study us, but to prepare our civilization for its awakening. What is this awakening?

This awakening is the spiritual progression of mankind towards the opening of his third eye and resulting peace that will come to your planet. It is through this awakening that mankind will have a fuller awareness of the Source and his connection to it. Mankind is meant to become the spiritual being he once was.

When will this awakening occur?

It depends on mankind, as there is free will in play, and it will not be a fast shift, but a gradual evolution. It may take centuries of your years or more. Evolution did not occur quickly, but evolved slowly at its own pace, and this shift also is a part of your evolutionary evolvement. The awakening will be gradual, and not all of mankind will experience it instantaneously, but each Source soul through humanity will experience it at various intervals. It is as a flower opens on a bush. Each flower opens at various times until they are all open.

There is much discussion lately, of the Mayan calendar coming to an end in 2012. Is the year 2012 connected, in any way, to this awakening?

Yes, it is connected, and this awakening will accelerate at this time so that more people will involve themselves. You must remember though, that there are more than six billion people on your planet, and this is why we say that it could take centuries. Evolution takes time.

What changes will take place in society as this shift progresses?

There will be a more caring unity between mankind, and there will be a level of attunement between the races, sexes, and cultures, but most importantly, there will be an attunement of the diverse religions as mankind begins to understand the true nature of God and his spiritual connection to the Source as a whole.

Can you tell us more about how our visitors are preparing mankind for its awakening?

They are communicating with various people who are, in turn, communicating with others through various means such as books, radio, and television, as well as word of mouth. They are communicating the state of the planet and the destruction that will occur if mankind continues on his current course. It is no different than what we are communicating through this book.

What other tools besides meditation can we utilize to promote the awakening of our third eye?

Meditation is very important, but there certainly are other avenues that can be utilized as well. We would recommend the practice of yoga and tai chi, for these practices focus the mind on the energy flow within your bodies. This is a good tool. Also, abstain from eating red meat, for this is not compatible with your body, and it causes a heaviness within your body that diverts its essential energies to the processing of a food substance that does not agree with your body. It is also beneficial to find time that causes a meditative state that eases stress.

You are here in this capacity because there is an awakening of humanity, and there is to be a determination to go forth in a state of awareness that involves another sense of perception. This is happening to a handful of people, and it is growing as a result of greater communication and acceptance that is available today. In the past, you would have been imprisoned or burned alive at the stake, but now in this time, cooler heads prevail, and there is more acceptance of these gifted people. Police forces have utilized these methods in their investigations, and this is but one example of the growing acceptance of these individuals. You are not crazy; you are quite sane. You are a glimpse of Earth's future development, and it is a slow development, but it will prevail.

Those that have these gifts will utilize them and use them for the greater good of themselves and mankind. There are messengers among you who are writing books such as this one, and are attempting to help to open the third eye of mankind. Those of you who are ready will be utilized by us for this purpose.

This book began as one page on meditation a number of years ago. We felt that these individuals were ready, and we took over one day in 2004. After a hiatus of many years, Tina and Tilde felt they were ready to channel the remainder of this book, and we are here to give mankind the insight it is ready to receive. Messengers don't always know their purpose until the time is upon them, and such was the case here. Many more messengers will appear, and many more books will be written. This book is one of many that Tina and Tilde will write.

Em: You are living in a time of great transformation and a time of accelerated learning. It is our intention to guide you through this phase of development as you awaken the sleeping giant within your organic body. Make an effort to meditate every day, and this will help to open the third eye of your soul. Everyone must realize that through meditation, your soul will experience an opening of mind and experience. We are here to help those of you who take this journey upon yourselves. There is a multitude of us who are ready to help those of you who undertake this spiritual quest. Meditate, and we will be there to help you as you embark upon this spiritual journey.

The awakening we speak of is simply mankind's graduation to the next level of his evolution. It entails an opening of his awareness with regards to his divinity and his natural state of being; that being a spiritual extension of the Source. Mankind is learning that his methods have not served him well and his differences have caused strife and misery. He is beginning to search for answers, and in his search, he is discovering that there is an alternate route towards an alternate reality.

Melanie: Your awakening has been in progress for many decades, but it has been accelerating as more of you are becoming aware of your spirituality and are opening yourselves to the ways of spirit through the Source. Many of you are questioning reality and wondering if there is more to life than what is sensed through your senses. Your journey is not by accident, but it is simply part of mankind's natural evolution.

When we spoke of the Source's quest for self-actualization, we spoke of how the Source first experienced instinct and emotion before conscious thought was added to the mix. It is now time for the next step, and it is time to open what you refer to as your sixth sense. When we speak of the third eye of humanity, we are speaking of this sixth sense. It is your natural evolution towards self-awareness and integration with the Source.   Make it a habit to meditate every day; and we cannot stress this enough.

As mankind awakens, he will discover his divinity and interconnectedness with one another and all of existence. He will realize that his way has not served him well, and that to destroy another is to destroy himself as well, for in this connectedness he will see himself in everything. As mankind awakens, he will see that love and peace will lead him to greater accomplishments and greater heights as he journeys through his evolution. He will come to understand magnetism and the laws of his Universe, and he will learn to manipulate his world and the reality he lives within. As a result of his next phase of evolution, he will cause himself to vibrate at a higher level, but he will, at this time, still retain his mass and density.

Your vibrational change will expand your awareness and your Universe, for it will allow friendly relations with the visitors who now conceal their identities from you. Your evolution is necessary because there are those among you who are not evolved, and they hold the balance of power through ignorance, greed, and the thirst for power and control. They will not prevail as you awaken, for the masses will speak and have their way when the time arrives. There is much strife and imbalance in your world, and this thirst for power blinds those who hold it. They are contributing to the destruction of your planet, which will lead to the destruction of the species that inhabit it. This is why your visitors are here. They seek to give you understanding and they seek to help you. They realize the interconnectedness of All That Is, including you. They seek to make you realize that by destroying yourselves, you also affect the Universe around you. They know that mankind has a destructive nature, but they are also aware of the seeds planted deep within your DNA that have not rooted yet. When mankind undergoes his transformation, it will alter your DNA; and this has been going on since your arrival on this planet. If you were to study the DNA of early man, it would differ somewhat from yours. As you evolve, your DNA will also evolve, and this will cause a greater form of mankind; one that is growing closer to his divine and rightful nature. Meditate every day.

What kinds of changes are taking place within our DNA as we evolve?

Your DNA has evolved as man evolved, and it will continue to do so as you continue to evolve. Your DNA will change to reflect the changes within you as it has always done. Who and what you are is encoded in your DNA. As you have evolved, this DNA code has evolved to reflect these changes. This is the case for all life forms on Earth. Your DNA is your blueprint. Think of it as a blueprint for the house you dwell within. As the structure of your house changes, the blueprint changes to reflect these alterations. If you add a room to your house, your blueprint will change to reflect this addition. Such is your DNA, which is the blueprint of the body that houses your soul.

Your Earth needs your help, and this awakening will guide you to the direction you must take. Your future is meant to be a bright one, for when the Source wanted to experience itself, it did so out of love; therefore, you must carry forth this legacy that is rightfully yours. Make it a habit to meditate and journey towards the spiritual fulfillment of your destiny. Let not those with closed minds rule you into doom and damnation, for this is a state of the lowest order, and those who hold onto this negative self greed do not fully understand the consequences of their laws and thinking. They will one day become the minority as mankind continues to awaken his spirit. Make this your goal.

We would urge you all to embark on a journey of spirituality and awareness. We would urge you all to alter your current course and take yourselves and this planet on a new course of healing and growth.

Just because you shift your awareness, does not mean that you must give up your luxuries and good life. You can still have these things and lead a spiritual and aware life. There is enough for everyone, and you need not fear loss of the things that you enjoy. Religion has disempowered you and taken your self awareness away. It has separated you from God by making you *think* that you are separate from God. Religion has controlled you through fear of the consequences. There are only the consequences that you hold in your mind.

I can see this last statement offending some people.

The truth is not always easy to digest. Just as governments control the countries they rule, so do religions control their parishioners through misinformation about the true nature of God. Jesus said it best when he said he was the

Son of God. He tried to impart the knowledge that we are all children of God, and that we must love each other because we are all brothers and sisters. Religion has at times ruled through fear and intimidation, but the Source is not to be feared. The Source is not a tool of intimidation. There are many who attend services on a Sabbath day, yet because they feel that they are absolved on each Sabbath, they go out and harm their brethren on the remaining days of the week. This is hypocritical of the human condition that religious beliefs can spawn. You are all children of God every day, and therefore, you should make every day seem like the Sabbath day that you observe.

Our next chapter is called.......

Chapter Fourteen:

Hell

Melanie: There is no hell other than the hell you have created for yourselves, and there is no devil other than the devil you have created for yourselves. This concept is so simple that our chapter should end here, but we realize the need for explanation.

You have lived in a world of heaven and hell, and this has been created by none other than yourselves. Hell is that mythical place where you believe that all bad and evil souls reside in. You believe that all bad and evil people go to hell when they die. They do not go to hell, for hell is a creation of the imbalanced mind and soul. When a soul is so attached to the belief system that was implanted upon it, this soul will, upon death, experience the reality of its own creation. If you believe in hell and you believe that you are going to hell, then upon your death you will experience the reality that you yourself have created. The hell that you experience is your version of what hell is. Remember when we spoke of thoughts having energy and creating their own reality through belief systems, well this applies to hell as well.

Are you saying that even though hell does not really exist, if you believe that you are going to hell, then you will experience exactly that when you die?

Yes. Make it a part of your meditation to alter your beliefs about the existence of hell. What you believe is what you create when you enter the spiritual realm. If you believe that you are going to hell, then you will experience a hell of your own making.

During your time on Earth, your religions have created a method of control through fear and intimidation. Their purpose was power and control, but in actuality, this purpose was to gain great wealth through power and control. They created the illusion of a judgmental God, but what good is a judgmental God if there are no consequences that follow if one is not obedient to the laws of church and state. A judgmental God is weakened without the threat of hell and the devil. How perfect a plan with which to control the masses. You do not need to believe this any more if you are to awaken your third eye, for it is an ignorant state that the awakened person does not accept or relate to. You are reaching a transformation that has no place for hell and the devil. Make no mistake about it; we urge you to discard the ancient and outdated concept of hell and its ruler.

If religions created hell and a judgmental God, what does this say about our religions? Are they bad?

No, not necessarily. We are more concerned about those religious cults who would brainwash their members and lead them to acts such as mass suicides, which you are aware of on your planet. Religions have a good message in their core, which is the acceptance of a Divine Source, but even religions must survive on this planet, and their methods have been heinous at times. The Spanish Inquisition would be an example of this.

Em: Hell is a creation of the humans in power who would seek to control the masses through fear. If you believe in hell and you believe that you will go there upon your physical death, then you will experience a hell of your own creation. Did you think that God would really be judgmental in his quest for self-actualization? The Source, in its desire to know itself, wanted to experience all that it is, and to be judgmental is to deny its quest. Remember that we told you that even though hate is an emotion of the lowest order, it still has its place, for how can you value love if you have not experienced hate? Hell exists in your mind, but because thoughts have energy, your thoughts have imbued it with a reality of your own creation.

If you would suspend your beliefs around organized religion, you would be able to understand its concept and purpose. It is called organized for a reason. We do not wish to impart the idea that all religion has led you astray. We wish to impart unto you that there are loving and caring religions that care about you. Trust your instincts, and listen to those religions whose message about the Source is pure and loving, for these religions will lead you towards the spirituality that is your heritage. Banish your beliefs about hell, and focus your beliefs on love and light, for this is your Source.

But doesn't evil exist? What about demons and evil spirits? What about hauntings and possessions? Where does all this fit in?

The hauntings that many of you experience are a result of lost souls who have not found their way to the Source upon a physical death. This is for many various reasons. Some souls feel that they have sinned and will not be accepted, so they are Earthbound. Some souls do not believe in anything after death, and this causes them to be Earthbound, and other souls may have left their bodies so violently and quickly that they do not even know that they are dead. As for what you term demons, these souls are negative entities that hold much anger and are Earthbound. They do not know how to release their hatred and anger, and this causes much pain and discomfort. If these angry souls would accept a loving Source and allow their anger to dissipate, they would find their way home. Sometimes, these souls are so attached to these emotions that they do not know how to begin to let go. They can only achieve unity with the Source if they would be willing to let this anger dissipate. Sometimes, these Earthbound angry souls attach themselves to the energy of people, and this is the reason for what you term a haunting or possession.

Is there any guidance for these lost souls? Are they eventually led back to the light, or are they left on their own?

Many are left until they discover that this way no longer works for them. Even this level of existence is a path of learning.

If hell does not exist, then what would stop people from committing criminal acts or harming other people? If hell does not exist, there is no deterrent.

Hell has never stopped criminals before; therefore, why should this change anything now?

If evil people do not go to hell, then where do they go?

They go to a deprogramming station, as you would term it, and they are assisted by guides and teachers who would assist in reviewing their lives on Earth and lessons learned. Do not forget that some of these evil people have their own journeys and lessons, and even these people are on their own learning paths in their attempts to find the Source.

There are entities who are lost as a result of their misguided beliefs. They do exist, and they are at times attracted to your light, but at no time do these entities reside in a hell that is not of their own making. You would do yourself much harm if you were to focus on hell and not the true heaven that is your heritage.

If upon physical death, you experience the hell you have created through your belief systems, what will happen to you if you never alter your beliefs? Will you experience an eternity of hell?

No, for many of these souls, in this time of distress, will usually call for God. We hear these souls and attempt to guide them to the light. There are many of us here whose purpose it is to help these souls eventually find their way home. Many of them find the light and then continue on their journeys of learning, for even in the darkness there are lessons to be learned.

Your experiences with the hell concept have been with you for centuries in their many different versions of the underworld. At first, this was a result of common ignorance on the matter. Humans did not fully understand the line between humanity and the other side. They attached their own beliefs to the underworld, and it evolved into hell. At first, the underworld was simply the world of death and spirit, but as it evolved, mankind became fearful of that which it could not see. Theories were developed, and as mankind evolved, these theories evolved, and in the hands of organized religion, they became tools of control.

If mankind chooses to believe in hell, then mankind will experience that which it creates through its belief systems. You think that all bad people are punished by God and go to hell. It appears to *us* that you worship an angry and hypocritical God. Love is the essence of God, and the essence of love does not allow anger and hatred to overrule it. Love overpowers hatred and love overpowers anger. The light is not extinguished by darkness. The light thrives and puts out the darkness with its light. Such is the essence of the Source.

You may be appalled to learn that those who you would put in hell have experienced the light of the Source upon a physical death. If they, who believe not in hell, leave their bodies, upon death, they will not experience hell. Hell is a part of your belief system. It is not a part of your true heritage. Your hell, you alone have created, and you alone dwell in the hell you have created. Your hell will appear as you believe it to exist. If you want to leave the hell of your own creation, then we would urge you to alter your belief and seek the Light.

Melanie: You have been misguided in your spiritual quest by some of the religions that you have followed and adhered to. Your views of hell are outdated and no longer serve your new awakening. Your time has come, and with this time there has also come the need to discard old belief systems that no longer serve mankind. It is time to put hell to bed forever. It is necessary for your development and growth. Make sure you do this, and make your future quest serve your awakening. Hell is obsolete. It does not exist, and it always gives negative connotations to God, for the Source is not judgmental. The Source is solely interested in your growth, development, and self-actualization. The Source has infinite love for you, and that does not accommodate a place called hell.

Karma is connected to your energy and belief system. Karma is not a tool of this hell that you have created. You would love to believe that karma dictates that all bad souls would be justly punished in hell. Karma is attached to your magnetism and works like the law of attraction. If your energy is negative, it will attract, through magnetism, negative situations. Many would label this karma, but in actuality, it is magnetism. Positive thoughts and beliefs attract positive situations, and again, many of you refer to this as good karma. In actuality, this is magnetism. Magnetism attracts that which your energy and belief systems create, so therefore, one might refer to magnetism as karma. Magnetism is neither positive nor negative. It is simply electrical energy, and electrical energy is magnetism. People have negative or positive thoughts and beliefs, and magnetism responds in like.

Em: Your version of karmic debt is wishful thinking and a hope for revenge for those who you think have caused great harm to others. Make no mistake about it; karma is magnetism in motion.

Hell is not real, and your version of hell is a place of karmic debt for those who you deem evil or bad. Each soul has a purpose, even those who you would deem evil. Souls who live in this evil reality have come here for a specific purpose, and this is at times for the growth of other souls. They have undertaken a great mission, and these souls do not take this mission lightly. Some of these souls who you would deem evil, have high regard in heaven, for their mission is an important one, and at times their evil deeds served to open mankind's awareness and shift the course of your world. These souls understood their purpose and did not take their missions lightly. They understood that their purpose was to serve the greater good of mankind through the lessons that were necessary to impart upon mankind. Their return to the Source did not include what you would term as hell. They earned a great respect, for their missions were honorable for the greater good of mankind's evolution, so you see, hell would serve no purpose to punish a noble cause. You always think that there must be negative consequences, but if you would see the bigger picture, you would understand the lessons learned and their delivery. Hell does not exist.

I think it is going to be very difficult for people to accept that evil souls have high regard in heaven. I, myself, am having a difficult time with this. Can you please explain this in such a way that we can begin to make sense of it?

Many souls who have journeyed to your dimension, have done so for the purpose of mutual learning through a shared event, and the soul who took on the responsibility to be that person who inflicted much pain, did so to assist in the mutual learning by playing out his own role, just as an actor would play a role on stage. We all have played many roles in our reincarnational journeys, but this does not mean that when we played evil roles our essence was evil. It means that we cooperated in a shared mutual event by assuming our part in the drama. Make no mistake that when these souls all crossed over, there was a remembrance of the agreement to share in the event, right down to the role of the so called evil one, and when all souls met on our side, there was much love between all of them. You do not lose the love and respect of your fellow players if you chose the evil role, for this is a very difficult decision for a loving soul to undertake.

Would a very evolved soul take on a role such as this, or is it generally less evolved souls that take on these roles?

No, not necessarily. The soul who would take on this role, would be a soul who was drawn to the lesson for his spiritual growth and development. Sometimes, highly evolved souls will take this mission, for they understand the gravity of it. This does not mean to diminish the gravity of the situation on Earth, for we recognize that as humans, there would have been suffering involved. Sometimes, these mass events are meant for the greater learning of those people who are not directly involved in the event. Sometimes, these events are meant to teach the rest of the planet a lesson of learning and spiritual growth.

If karmic debt is wishful thinking, then how do you explain the theory of reincarnating for the purpose of clearing a previous karmic debt?

It is simply reincarnating to learn a lesson that was missed or to repeat a life to repeat the lesson from a different perspective. What you term as karma, is actually magnetism in motion. When we say that someone is receiving bad karma because of a bad deed, this bad deed is attracting the bad energy due to what you term as the law of attraction, which is what we term as magnetism. Karma is a name that you have given it; therefore for you, karma exists because your belief system has drawn the energy into existence, but in reality it is magnetism.

So we can repeat the same life?

We are speaking of probable realities when we speak of repeating a life from a different perspective, but to repeat the exact same life would indeed be redundant. In order to learn a lesson, we experience a reincarnational life, and this life is filled with probabilities depending on our beliefs and decisions. They expand exponentially depending on these decisions and paths that we take.

Meditate, and your awareness and understanding will expand. It is time for you to reach the next level of your rightful heritage. MEDITATE. In capitals. Your time has come and your higher self awaits you.

Demna: Heaven is our next chapter.

Hell

Chapter Fifteen:

Heaven

Demna: Heaven exists, and it is our home. It is where each soul longs to return to, and it is a place of exquisite love and light.

When the Source yearned to leave and journey, it sent out extensions of itself from the place of love and light, and its quest included a return home at intervals throughout this quest. Each soul is an extension of the Source, and each soul has its own separate identity as well as its connection to the Source. It is as each cell within your body has its own identity, yet is still connected to you. It has a dual personality and existence while being a part of the one identity. Such are you. Your body is but the organic shell that houses your soul while it journeys in this current reality. Your soul has a personality that is individual, yet merged with the Source.

When you exit your body upon a physical death, your soul retains the identity it had in this life, but it also retains every identity it has ever held. You will never cease to be you. You will always remember this life, and it can never be extinguished. Your other lives can never be extinguished. Think of your life today, and think of the number of jobs you held. Each job is still a part of you, and each job did not annihilate your past when you took on a new job. Such is the journey of your soul. Think of your past lives in this manner, and you will understand what we say.

You state that when we exit our bodies we retain our identities and any identity we've ever had. Do we also retain our relationships with our parents, grandparents, etc?

(I would like to note here, that during the writing of this book we would occasionally be visited by an entity who referred to herself as Mama. From what she has told us, Tina and I were brothers living in Italy during the Renaissance in the 1500's. She was our mother at that time and continues to watch over us, even now. She comes through periodically, during our sessions, and each time, makes a point of telling us how much she loves us and how proud of us she is. I suppose it is only fitting that she would come through to answer this particular question for us.)

Mama: You do retain all of your relationships with all of your friends and family because these people were a part of your lives on Earth, and these important relationships carry on into heaven. You also retain relationships with those on Earth who may have been your enemies, but in heaven these souls are now your friends.

Demna: Life is a journey, and when it is over, you return back to your home base. This home is the home you left behind when you embarked on this journey of your current self. When you leave this Earth, you return to this home. You are sometimes met, upon death, by a friend or relative who guides you out of your body, and you may not know that you have just died because it is so real and there is no pain or discomfort associated with this passing. Others may find themselves, at once, thrust out of their bodies where they might be disoriented and confused. You will be drawn to a light, and this light is heaven calling you home. Make sure that you understand this, for you will all come home one day. We are here to greet you, and there will be many friends and relatives you knew who will be anxiously and lovingly awaiting your arrival. To us, it is cause for much celebration. We are happy to have you back home.

Many of us are very fearful of dying. We are afraid that it will be painful, and we are afraid of the unknown.

Melanie: We understand this, but remember that there is no unknown because heaven *is* known and very real. As far as painful deaths go, remember that many sudden deaths are but a brief moment and then it is done, and you have crossed. Some deaths are so sudden that there is no pain felt, and some souls do not immediately know that they are dead. In fast tragedies, some people who survive, do not even sense pain immediately, and some of you have predetermined your manner of death for the learning that it imparts. The anxiety over death and pain is understandable, but the anticipation of what may be is actually worse than the event itself. We would like to alleviate this anxiety. You have died many times, yet here you are today, experiencing life again.

What if we die and we don't feel we're ready yet? What if we feel that we still have unfinished business here? Do we have a choice in the matter?

Source: We are Source. You all have reasons for your journeys, and all have the desire to stay. It is a natural function of the ego to survive, for if not, then many of you would not choose to stay in your physical bodies, and simply take your own lives, for the desire to return home would be so great. The ego serves as a method to keep the soul rooted within the body, so it is natural to not want to die a physical death. Having said that, it is still within the soul's determination to have and exercise free will, and this reality can be altered so that death can be postponed, but death will not be postponed unless the soul has determined a greater cause and path which allows it more time in the physical body.

Heaven is your home, and it is everything good that you would want your home to be. As within, so without. Heaven represents all that is good in your life, and it is not always easy to leave home and embark on a journey, but embark we must, for each journey brings growth, lessons, and greater awareness.

I am familiar with 'as above, so below', but you often say 'as within, so without.' Is the meaning the same?

Make sure that you understand that within, lies the Source and without, lies the external representation of the Source. What is occurring within you becomes expressed and realized without you. Without, meaning externally.

When we greet you, once you have departed your physical body, we give you an orientation of your life on Earth. This is referred to by many of you as your life flashing before your eyes. It does happen, but it is not a judgmental thing, as many of you believe it to be. It is a review of your life and the lessons learned while there. It is a reflection of your life, and its purpose is to further your awareness and to jog your soul's memory as to why these events occurred.

There is a time to reflect and a time to ask questions if you so desire. There may be souls in heaven that came here before you, and these souls have been on your journey with you. Some souls learned these lessons with you, and this is a good time for you to reflect together and learn together what the purpose was for your mutual events.

If you are a soul who we spoke of, whose journey was for the good of mankind and you took on the so called evil role, then this is a time to deprogram you and restore your soul's divinity. At times, you will feel the emotions of those you affected, whether these emotions are good, bad, sad, and so forth. Because we are all connected, it cannot be any other way, for each emotion is a part of the whole, and therefore, is felt by the whole. By feeling the emotions of those you have affected, it causes you to also learn their lessons because in being a part of the whole, all is a mutually shared event, therefore, each lesson you learn is also learned by us all.

You say that each lesson we learn, is learned by us all. If this is the case, then why aren't we all equally evolved?

Because of our separate journeys and lessons. It is a journey that is individual to each Source soul, yet felt by all Source souls, for we are all connected.

Hmmm......

We see you don't understand. It is quite simple. Each Source soul has its own lessons to learn, and each Source soul is on its own individual learning curve. We are learning our lessons in different ways, but because we are connected, each experience is felt by the whole of the Source because the Source is experiencing all through you. When the Source birthed all that is, it did not create separation. As a result, everything is experienced by the whole on what you term the spiritual level; like the events on Earth are broadcast, and therefore, realized by all of humanity even though they are not directly involved in the event. You have seen the images of devastation on the news when a tornado or hurricane occurs. You experience the event vicariously through those effected. Meditate on this concept to understand the full impact of what we say.

Em: Heaven is your true home, and your journey away from home is always filled with the certainty that you will return. It is always a short journey in comparison to the everlasting now, and that is what makes it easier for each soul to leave. It is the knowledge that you will always return here.

When you return home and your life has been reviewed, many of you will go through an orientation session and your memories of all of your existence will be restored. It is akin to a home coming, but in a grander scale. Some of you will rest a while and some of you will continue your lessons immediately, while others might want to continue exploring heaven. There is much to do here, and you will never get bored or stop learning. Make no mistake about it; heaven does exist and it is a very full, and rich, and loving environment.

For those who continue exploring heaven, what could they see and do in heaven?

There are many temples of learning in heaven, and these temples can be attended by any soul who wishes to attend. There are gardens to visit and Universes to discover, and souls who visit with each other. There are souls, such as ourselves, who wish to educate mankind, and we do work such as this work through you. There is music and choirs that sing God's praises. There are discoveries occurring in heaven that are imparted to those on Earth through divine inspiration. There are experiences and vistas that you can create through your soul mind, and there are many mansions that can be viewed and lived in. There is so much beauty and possibilities, that we can go on forever explaining them to you, but this is what you can begin to glimpse in heaven.

Many of you think that when you die you simply cease to exist, as if your light were simply extinguished. This is so wrong and nowhere near the truth of your post death journey. Death is simply a term for an end of a phase, but it is a birth into another level of existence. Birth and death are synonymous, and a death in one plane signifies a birth into another plane. You can never be destroyed. Your energy is simply transformed from one level to another.

Melanie: By birth, we mean a transformation from heaven to Earth. By death we mean a transformation from Earth to heaven.

Heaven is a place of brilliance and love. By brilliance, we mean that it is of the white light, but also that everything that exists here is much more brilliant and richer than anything on Earth. When you die, you merge with the white light of the Source from whence you came, but do not confuse the meaning of this. We do not mean that your soul is absorbed by the light and merged into an existence of one separate identity. We mean that the white light, that is your home, welcomes you back and opens its door so that you may enter. You will still be you, and you will not lose your identity.

As within, so without. This has greater meaning than you know. Everything that is good on Earth may also exist in heaven, but it is richer and more brilliant than on Earth. Music exists in heaven. All of the music that has been composed on Earth existed in heaven first, but in heaven it is more beautiful than the music heard on Earth. When music is translated to the Earth plane, it loses its brilliance through the denser vibrations of Earth. You are aware of many beautiful melodies that you hear on Earth, but these melodies have a richer and more beautiful resonance when heard in heaven. Make heaven a part of your meditation and you may receive glimpses of your home.

Demna: Your Earthly version of heaven is but a small view of what heaven is. You call it heaven, but we call it home. Home is where we all come from, and home is a part of the Source, just as we all are. Home is within the Source and a part of the Source. When we said "as within, so without," it is in a sense quite literal, as all that ever will exist already does exist within the Source. Everything that you create on Earth already exists in the ether of All That Is. Heaven has many facets that are more beautiful than Earth. The flowers that you will find in heaven are more beautiful and fragrant than those on Earth. Every animal that exists on Earth exists in heaven, and the beings that inhabit heaven are loving and gentle souls that glow with the brilliance of the white light, for we are made of white light, and we are the white light.

I don't mean to keep going back to this, but just as I thought I was beginning to understand the concept of the Universe's expansion, you state that "all that ever will exist, already does exist within the Source." Doesn't "all that ever will exist" include the expanding now? And if so, doesn't this mean that the Source is already self-actualized?

Make sure you listen carefully. Everything that will ever exist, already exists within the mind of the Source, but in concept only until it is realized through actualization of experience.

In a material sense?

Yes. The Universe is expanding because as each experience or concept is actualized physically, it remains as a concept first, and once it is experienced, it takes form in your three dimensional world.

And is this what you mean by, "the now is always expanding?"

Yes. It is like having many seeds that have not sprouted yet, and when they sprout, they contribute to the expansion.

We have always been, and we will always be. There is no beginning as you know it, and there is no end. There is just the everlasting now, and heaven is a part of the everlasting now. Everything that exists in heaven is good, and we are all a part of that goodness. Your buildings exist in heaven, but far more beautiful than you can imagine. Your houses exist in heaven, but far more beautiful than you can imagine. There are flora and fauna that exist in heaven just as on Earth, but the colors are richer, and deeper, and brighter than you know. Everything vibrates with the angelic sound of heaven, and music is permeating all with sound and feeling. We can only describe heaven to you in Earthly terms, but these terms are inadequate compared to the true splendor of heaven.

Melanie: Heaven is in the light of God. God does not exist in heaven; heaven exists in God. Your home is a part of All That Is, just as you are.

There are many levels of heaven, just as there are many levels on Earth. One level is not better than another, it is just different. There are different levels of being in heaven, and this is not to be construed as better or worse, it is just a different level of ascension, per se. When we first enter heaven, we go through a deprogramming and orientation. This is but a level of heaven. It is no less beautiful and loving than any other level. Think of it as a house with many rooms. No room is better than another, it is just another room. One room in your Earthly home is for dining, one is for sleeping, another is for bathing; so you see, it is not better, just different. When Jesus said that in heaven there are many mansions, this is what he spoke of. The levels are for different functions, and your soul may enter each level as it so desires for its purpose. There are levels of continued learning and growth, and there are levels of greater assimilation with the Source for the purpose of grand learning and all encompassing awareness.

You say that there are many levels of heaven, just as there are many levels on Earth. What do you mean by, many levels on Earth?

Making these parallels of levels is an attempt to make you understand that the levels on heaven exist just as levels on Earth exist. Think of it as a grade school with many levels of grades. As you finish one grade, you graduate onto the next grade. This is what we mean.

As within, so without. You see, Earth is but an attempted facsimile of heaven. Earth has its places of learning and its arenas of learning. Earth has its places of orientation just as heaven does, and Earth has its temples where one may try to become one within the Source. In heaven, these levels are simply grander, more beautiful, and purer than Earthly words can convey. You all have a place in heaven, for truly there is no hell; and we all are born of heaven, and we are all meant to find our way back home again. Levels that exist in heaven are for the benefit of all within the Source. It is a difficult concept to explain in Earthly terms without conveying a sense of separateness. There is no sense of separateness within heaven or the Source. There is only a feeling of the purest, deepest, love and unity, and joy. The essence of heaven is God's essence, and God's essence is heaven. It is All That Is, for to return to heaven is to return to God, for when you are in heaven, you reside within the God Source that birthed your soul and gave it free will and freedom to explore.

Em: Heaven is a very real existence, and it is more real than the one you currently reside in. Remember that your world and its probabilities are dreams of the Source for the purpose of self-actualization, and your souls are like offshoots of the dreaming mind. When the dream is over, the dreamer awakens. Such is the reality of life and its rebirth into heaven. Your arrival into heaven is akin to the awakening dreamer. You are a part of the dream that occurs on the dimension of Earth. It is the awakening of your soul as it reviews its dream experience on Earth and becomes reoriented with its true home and reality.

As your soul continues its orientation of heaven, you may decide to expand your consciousness in many ways. You may decide to reincarnate and live the dream illusion of Earth in another lifetime, or you may continue to explore the levels of heaven for further learning and reorientation. You have many friends in the house of God, and you are deeply attached to the house of God. This is why it is difficult to leave God and go back to Earth for many, and most, of the Source souls, but mankind's evolution is not complete, for the evolution of man is the evolution of the soul in its quest for the Source's self-actualization.

Can we decide to not reincarnate, and just live out the rest of our existence in heaven?

Yes, but you would not grow as a Source soul, for the experiences on Earth are a part of the Source's self-actualization of which you are a part. It is like not graduating from one grade to the next.

When we reincarnate, can we do so on another planet in another galaxy or Universe, or do we have to reincarnate back to Earth?

Many of you have reincarnated on other planets and have reincarnated this time on Earth to contribute to mankind's awakening. So you *can* reincarnate onto other planets, but many of you have preferences of location and choose to reincarnate on the same planet time and again. Many soul groups experience their lives together, and they have preferences of where they reincarnate. Mankind is not exclusive to reincarnating on Earth and has experienced other levels of existence. Your particular soul group prefers Earth the most.

What do you mean by soul group?

The soul group would include your parents, friends, relatives, and so forth. They also encompass your oversoul. Think of the soul group as a pod of souls who choose to experience a lifetime together. This group would be a part of an oversoul which would include a greater amount of soul portions of itself. Think of yourself as being an oversoul. All your cells would be a part of this oversoul, yet each would carry its own identity within the oversoul, and through the experiences of each cell, you as an oversoul share in the experiences. They are a part of you, yet separate, in so far as having their own identities, just as each soul retains his own identity within the Source.

Heaven is your home, and although you travel to your current realities in each lifetime, your home always awaits your return. Each Source soul is welcomed lovingly at the end of their journey, and each soul is guaranteed a place in heaven.

Demna: We will now embark on the final chapter. Your future.

Chapter Sixteen:

The Future of Mankind

Demna: Mankind is at a crossroads in his destiny, and there is much excitement among those of us who have journeyed with you as your guides and angels. We urge you to take the step that is your rightful heritage, and open the third eye of mankind. Mankind has reached a fork in the path of his destiny, and there is much upheaval in your world today. It is time to open the awareness that will lead to the discovery of your true legacy and future.

The planet cannot sustain you further in your current course, and there have been many among you who are heralding this message loud and clear. The Earth is fighting against its rape and pillage, and though you may think you are smart, your intelligence is pale in the presence of the Source's eye, as you stand three dimensionally upon this planet. If you do not open your third eye, you may cause your very extinction. This is a serious matter, and it does already exist as one of your probable realities. The other probable reality is the opposite of this; and in this other probable reality, mankind has opened his third eye and honors the Mother Earth that sustains his very existence.

Don't you get it? You are destroying that very Earth that sustains your life and existence. This is a serious matter, and we all have a vested interest in the survival of your species. It is not for mankind to evolve this way. Mankind's evolution should lead to an integration with the Source through ascension; through his development of his higher vibrational frequency.

I am Demna, and I will now lead this chapter.

You have only had glimpses of me throughout this book, but I have not been invisible throughout. I am as we are, and I and you are one with the Source of Light and Love, for it is through love that we bear this message.

Though there are many probable realities, the probable reality of your extinction is one that we would avoid in all cases of reality. We have seen all probabilities because where we stand, we can glimpse all results in the everlasting now. We would urge you to take the high road.

We do not wish to make you fearful. The course that you are currently on would lead to a path of destruction if left unchecked. When we speak of the devastation of the probability of mankind's extinction due to his ways, we speak of it as a distant future probability. It always can be altered. This probability is an occurrence that could happen in centuries, or thousands of your Earth years, but do not let this sway you into a false sense of security. The planet is polluted. It has a lowered capacity to pump out clean air, and the trees you are cutting down are further limiting their capacity. Reforestation cannot currently maintain pace for pace with the deforestation. You have only to do the math. One is creating an imbalance and the other cannot keep pace. Your oxygen is precious. What good is your capitalism if you are either too ill or dead to appreciate what you feel are the rewards.

We urge you to be logical and sensitive to the needs of your planet. If you are not sensitive to the needs of your planet, it will, in turn, not be sensitive to your needs. How can a barren mother supply milk for her child? It is a truth that you must address. The symptoms of your plunder are all around you. Your children have asthma. Your food is genetically engineered, and no longer has the life sustaining equivalence of the food your ancestors ate. The genetically engineered food is being stripped of its ability to produce seeds, and in the future you will be at the mercy of those corporations who seek to make you dependent solely on them for your sustenance. Food will be a luxury that the wealthy will be able to afford. The staples that will be stripped of their nutrients, is what the rest of mankind must survive on. It is becoming a corporate world that will control the government through its wealth, and lobbyists, and fine print.

You are becoming a species that is being manipulated by your corporations to serve their expanding greed for power, control, and domination. It is your choice whether to allow this or whether to make a difference through your peaceful free will. Make your life count. Make the lives of your future generations count. Be aware of the differences you can make for yourselves and this planet.

(We paused for a break here and began discussing the material that had just come through. We commented on how the reality of what was happening to our world, was almost beginning to sound like a science fiction movie where corporations were becoming living entities, and it was their mission to become as large as possible and ensure their survival by any means necessary. They would begin controlling the food supplies. All naturally growing food would become genetically modified so that it could no longer produce seeds, resulting in people no longer being able to grow their own food. In the future, people would be dependent on corporations for all their food. Would it be illegal to cultivate your own seeds in the future? Would all seeds have to come exclusively from the corporations? Makes for great science fiction. Unfortunately, the line between reality and science fiction is becoming blurred.)

We are impressed with your understanding, and we will continue.

Your major corporations are indeed entities unto themselves, and being thus, they are compelled to survive and expand in great leaps and without impediment. In order to do this, they must gain control of the consumer, and they must do this in order to maintain their longevity. Make no mistake; they will rule if allowed, and the ultimate power will not belong to the voter. The ultimate power will belong to the corporations of gluttony. They are as the children of your bible who worshipped golden idols while Moses took his leave of them to commune with God. Add but the letter "L" to God, and gold will become God.

There is nothing wrong with wealth. There is nothing wrong with wanting wealth. Money is neither good nor evil. Money is neutral. Man is the outcome of his actions in how he handles money. Man can have money, and wealth, and a sustainable, healthy planet and environment. He who loves deeply his planet, will help to sustain its health. We would urge you to love this planet in all its beauty and splendor. We would urge you to be the caretakers that you were meant to be when you began to inhabit this planet. Your dollars that you love so much can make a difference. You can control corporations with your money. Since money is neutral, it is up to you to leave your own neutral comfort zone, and put your money into those areas that would benefit you, your children, and your planet. Be not neutral, for neutrality will be mankind's downfall. Be involved. Be engaged, and be in love with Mother Earth.

We would urge you to become more responsible in your treatment of your planet. Your consumerism would be less harmful if you balanced it with a better approach towards discarding that which you consume. The planet is becoming a dumping ground of garbage that does not decompose. It is killing your wildlife who consume it, innocently. It is leaking dangerous chemicals into your soil and water. It is leaking noxious gasses into your atmosphere. Love your planet. It is the only one you have. Make it a habit to take care of that which sustains you. It can be reversed, but it will take effort on your part. Be engaged and be concerned. You can take the steps, but you must *want* to take them in order to turn the events around. Make every effort. We will guide you.

You can make a difference in your world, and you can do it by starting to take small steps at first. It does not take much to start. You can start simply by walking the short distances that you would normally drive. If everyone on this planet made that one simple adjustment, it would make a difference in the world wide emissions. Take it to the next step, and decide to walk to any destination that would take you no more than one half hour of walking time. This would not only alleviate emissions, but would contribute to the benefits of your health as well. Start walking.

When you must be mobile and use a vehicle, make decisions as to the type of vehicle you use. If you can, use public transportation instead of your car. If you must use a car, then think about the type of car you buy. There are more fuel efficient vehicles that you can buy these days. Not everyone can afford them, but if you can, it would be a better investment for your planet's future.

The corporations would be wise to develop fuel alternatives. At one time, there was experimentation with electric cars on a wider scale than now, but they threatened the corporations who were directly affected by these vehicles, and they were eliminated. It would be wise to reintroduce them. Your dependency on your current form of fuel is affecting your planet adversely, and it should be reversed. It *can* be reversed because the technology exists. If your corporations would let go of their fears, they would discover that they can make the transition safely and without great detriment to their bottom lines. It can be accomplished.

You have the capacity to create solar power to generate your electrical and energy needs. This would help greatly, for there would be an alleviation in the need to reroute your water to produce energy. Rerouting our water affects the delicate balance of nature in the affected areas, which affects the habitat and wildlife. Since all is interconnected, it affects mankind as well. Like it or not, you will pay the consequences one day.

Making adjustments in your daily lives will impact the Earth in a small but positive way, but your corporations are the major offenders. They do not adhere to many of the policies and rules that your governments have in place, and your governments lack the nerve to hold them accountable, and therefore, they get away with much that goes undetected by the public and powers that be. It is by their greed and by their major mistakes that some of these corporations fall to their demise. Enron is but one example of this greed and thirst for invincibility. *Then*, it is that the public discovers the gross negligence of these entities. There are many more, and they affect the well being of your planet. These corporations have the ability and power to set shining examples for change, but the greed and thirst that powers them, overrules any benefits that they could offer.

It is in the hands of the consumers, and if the consumers would begin to make wiser choices on how they spend their money, a change could be affected. Think carefully on where you spend your dollars. Start buying organic food that is not genetically altered in any way. In this way, you can begin to save your future food supplies and prevent the corporations from taking control and copyrighting that food which is rightfully yours. Yes, copyrighting; because the science behind it is owned by the corporations that develop it.

Start growing your own food. Start planting gardens again, and take back your God given food. It was given freely to you through this planet by your Creator and Source. Do *not* allow it to be taken away from you. It is *rightfully* yours.

There are many other steps you can begin to take. Your water is being purified and sold back to you. This is a resource that used to be clean and free. Be attentive to the water systems in your areas. Be aware of who the polluters are, and start to demand of your governments that they be held accountable. Together, many voices can become one, and many voices that do not let up can begin to affect changes in the laws and regulations. There are many corporations who are polluting your waters. There are many corporations that are polluting your oceans and polluting the fish and creatures who live in, and off, the ocean's inhabitants.

Your scientists are discovering plastics in the bellies of the animals that survive in the oceans. These plastics are discarded by all of you, in some manner or other. Begin to eliminate the use of plastics where you can, and when you use plastics, be conscientious in their disposal. Begin to recycle all of that which you use. Do not throw these items into garbage dumps. They do not decompose, and they will exist long after you are gone. You can recycle everything from plastic, to aluminum, to paper and beyond.

Start to be conscious of your actions on this planet, and begin to make adjustments. Educate yourself because knowledge is the power to understand a different way of living in, and of treating, your environment. Educate yourself in all the ways you can make a difference. Aerosols can be replaced by pump sprays. Just this one adjustment, adopted by everyone on this planet, can make a difference. Many small adjustments in everyone's lives can begin to have a cumulative affect on your planet. This is but a beginning. There are many other steps that mankind can take.

You are more empowered than you believe. Many of you coming together with one voice and one mutual activation, can make a difference; and it *will* make a difference if you try it. You only have to think of Gandhi and how he created evolutionary peaceful change by amassing the people in one unified peaceful voice. Make your voices unified.

The next phase of mankind should include a spiritual awakening, and if you engage in a true spiritual awakening and intellectual awakening, you will see how truly unified and connected you are as a spiritual species. There is no need for war and hatred in a truly spiritually unified species. It is a natural progression, and it will unify the world.

It is not mankind's destiny to be a warrior species, but it is one of your probable realities. If you maintain your current course of spiritual blindness along with personal and corporate greed, you will eventually extinguish yourself as a result of this. Your destiny is in your hands, and you must open your third eye of awareness. It is a necessity that will ensure the continuation of your species. Without the human species, this planet, along with its habitat, and animals, and nature, thrive quite well and unencumbered. It has been the addition of mankind and his conscious intelligence that has thwarted this great experiment of reality at this stage of evolution.

Your spiritual awakening will assist you in understanding the interconnectedness of All That Is and all that exists within All That Is. Mankind's awakening is a necessity, and it will lead mankind to a peaceful coexistence with all that exists on your planet. Be aware of the road that you are taking, for it is your destiny to inherit the Earth, but it must be a whole, and healthy, and peaceful Earth.

There are many cultures and religions that inhabit this planet. You can all coexist while respecting each other's differences. Your fear of each other causes and begets violence. You need not fear each other, for your differences are the results of the many different paths of learning that each soul is undertaking for a purpose of the Source's self-actualization. It is an honorable journey that each, and every one of you are on. Do not fight over your differences. It is acceptable to agree to disagree without hatred and violence. Allow each other the right to peaceful and respectful self awareness through each individual's journey. You do not need to fight or fear assimilation by one another. Live in love and peace, and allow each other to explore each person's lessons and journey. It is not a fearful thing to allow others their freedom and opinions.

Strive towards a peaceful, loving, and unified Earth. Strive towards a healthy Earth. Your planet has everything you require to survive and be healthy.

The drugs that are being developed are not necessarily in your best interests. Again, this is another area of your corporate greed. Illness is a business. Cures promote cessation of business. It is not logical to corporations to cure patients. It is logical to mask the symptoms so that medication can be purchased perpetually. It is in the interest of corporate medical greed to maintain and control the longevity of your illnesses. It is not in their best interest to cure you.

There was a time when medication was good and honest, but that time is gone for you. Go back to the Earth, and you will discover that the Source provided for all your needs, organically. The planet Earth has everything mankind requires for sustenance and healing. Go back to your natural Doctors, and go back to looking at your belief systems to discover the causes of your illnesses. There is more to it than meets the eye, as you would say.

We are not advocating that you eliminate modern medicine. We are trying to remind mankind of the connection he once had with Earth and all of its natural resources and remedies. They are as fruitful today as they were in your past history. If you would try, it would benefit you to seek natural remedies in conjunction, and addition to your modern medicine. You would be well advised to seek alternative medicines as well. Chinese medicine has many benefits that the western medical practitioners do not understand or believe in, but remember that the Chinese have a longer history than your western ones, and they have much to contribute to the western world. Seek out your Doctors of natural medicine in addition to your Doctors of western medicine.

We would urge you to seek change for mankind on many different levels. We have spoken of your food supply and your peaceful coexistence, as well as your spiritual growth and medicinal natural courses. It is up to you to take the first steps, but just as a baby learns to walk, you too will learn to walk on your new path of spiritual coexistence. As you take this new path, you will discover your bright future awaiting you.

At this time, you are at a fork in mankind's path, and we urge you to take the peaceful and loving way. It is up to you. Your future should be a peaceful one, and your path should lead to the coexistence with one another through peaceful interconnectedness with, and through, the Source. If not, then mankind will continue to lead a path of violence, hatred, fear, and destruction. This is not the enlightened way.

We would wish you much love and peaceful coexistence.

Afterword

Melanie: Many of you might still be determining whether or not to believe that a book can actually be channeled through a Ouija board, let alone a book that is extensive, as this is. We would advise that even though the method may appear outrageous, put your thoughts aside, and heed the message we impart, for you must admit it is indeed a loving, yet powerful message we bring. We have much love for you because as kindred spirits, our bonds go deeper than any Earthly bonds you will ever know.

Heed our message and take our advice to heart, for the heart is where God dwells and makes his home inside of each and every one of you.

We would wish you much love and growth for the betterment of the human species, and we will walk beside you as you travel the journey of your soul's desire. We are never far; and if you call upon us, we will speak through the God within your soul, and we will never let you down or steer you wrong. In the stillness of your soul, you will find us. We are simply waiting for you to awaken the spirit within.

Go in peace and love, and know that we will meet again.

CPSIA information can be obtained at www.ICGtesting.com
Printed in the USA
LVOW111412290312

275304LV00003B/176/P

9 780981 314501